SOUTH AFRICA'S
GREAT WHITE
SHARK

Text by
THOMAS P PESCHAK
MICHAEL C SCHOLL

D1509502

Photographs by
THOMAS P PESCHAK

Struik Publishers
(a division of New Holland Publishing
(South Africa) (Pty) Ltd)
Cornelis Struik House
80 McKenzie Street
Cape Town 8001

New Holland Publishing is a member of
Johnnic Communications Ltd.
Visit us at www.struik.co.za
Over 40 000 unique African images
available to purchase from our image
bank at www.imagesofafrica.co.za

First published in 2006

10 9 8 7 6 5 4 3 2 1

Publishing manager: Pippa Parker
Managing editor: Rod Baker
Editors: Helen de Villiers, Cisca Vennard
Design director: Janice Evans
Designer: Robin Cox
Proofreader: Joanna Ward
Indexer: Mary Lennox

Reproduction by Hirt & Carter Cape (Pty) Ltd
Printed and bound by Craft Print International Ltd

ISBN: 1 77007 382 5
Barcode: 9781770073821

To Samantha, thank you for your love, friendship, inspiration and understanding – and just simply for putting up with me.
THOMAS P PESCHAK

CONTENTS

FOREWORD

Being at the top draws heat. Think about the Chief Executive Officer (CEO) of any large corporation, or the coach of a major sports team. For such incumbents, one mistake negates years of strong leadership and countless judicious decisions. And yet it's no overstatement to say that our country's future relies largely on the wise, principled leadership of these captains of industry.

Things appear to be no different in our oceans. Sharks are top predators and can be seen as the CEOs of Oceans Inc. And, not unlike any large corporation, they oversee a number of business divisions: the service division, comprised mostly of fish stocks that continue to provide food and livelihoods despite ongoing abuse at the hands of greedy clients; the rather flamboyant marketing division, which includes all those 'pretty species' that flaunt their gaudy feathers, fins or scales to entice clients; and finally the operations division, blessed neither with good looks nor fortitude, but providing those important ecological linkages and supporting environment that enable the entire system to function.

But I have omitted one vital component of Oceans Inc. – the shareholders. According to the relevant legislation, all South African citizens are shareholders in the South African chapter of Oceans Inc. The bottom line: if Oceans Inc. (South Africa) goes belly up, to harness an insensitive pun, we're all going to lose big time.

So how is Oceans Inc. doing at the moment? Not well at all, frankly. The service division has suffered a massive blow with the overexploitation of 75% of our commercial fish stocks. But perhaps the most worrying aspect is the demise of the executive capacity (or CEOs) of the corporation. Ninety per cent of all top predators – mainly sharks – have been removed from our oceans through irresponsible management, greatly diminishing the functioning of these ecosystems.

Recently some of South Africa's most experienced marine biologists met to discuss the future of the Great White Shark: how to manage Great Whites while also ensuring the safety of recreational ocean users in the Western Cape. The experts not only agreed that the Great White Shark is an invaluable component of healthy marine ecosystems, but also that measures such as the installation of shark nets or culling of sharks were not desirable. Complete reliance on non-lethal methods was suggested. The 'shark-spotter programme', started by volunteer groups and NGOs, relies on people stationed at high vantage points to warn bathers of the presence of sharks.

Among many other recommendations, the experts also recognised the need to de-sensationalise the public's fear of sharks, and shatter the many myths surrounding shark behaviour and their infrequent interactions with humans. *South Africa's Great White Shark* is a scientifically solid, yet inspiring book which does exactly that.

I spend much time in the sea, perhaps more than my family or employers are comfortable with. So am I scared of sharks? Like other CEOs, sharks do make occasional mistakes which are met with much sensationalism and vilification. But statistics tell me that I'm more likely to be wiped out on the way to the beach by one of my fellow drivers than to encounter a shark in the ocean and be mistaken as prey. We fear most that which we do not understand. This book will help us understand, admire, respect and co-exist with one of most awesome creatures in our oceans – the Great White Shark.

Dr Deon Nel, WWF Sanlam Marine Programme

PREFACE

More than 100 species of shark inhabit South Africa's two oceans, yet it is the Great White that instantly comes to mind whenever the word shark is mentioned. As marine biologists and underwater photographers working with Great White Sharks, we are often asked probing questions about our work and the creature we have chosen to study. How big do Great Whites get? Why do they jump out of the water? Do people get bitten because they look like seals? Does chumming cause shark bites? Are Great Whites threatened by extinction? Is cage diving dangerous? The desire for knowledge about Great Whites appears to be endless and, whether driven by fear or fascination, the interest in these creatures is on the increase.

Accurate information is hard to come by and is limited to the occasional voice of reason buried amongst sensational newspaper pieces written in the wake of shark-bite incidents. It is therefore not surprising that many people still believe the Great White to be nothing more than a ruthless killing machine. This popular portrait, however, is foreign to us. In our experience, we find Great White Sharks to be curious, powerful, sleek, cautious, beautiful, intelligent, and even playful.

Taking into account its size, perceived ferocity and international notoriety, one would expect there to be countless scholarly volumes on every facet of the Great White Shark's life, from birth to death. Oddly, just the opposite is true. In South Africa, the world's Great White hot spot, where large numbers of sharks occur at very accessible study locations, scientific research only got underway in the mid 1990s. As a result, most of the research findings have not yet worked their way into popular literature, and some are so new that they have not even been published scientifically. As a result the public has only had access to outdated or simplistic information, often pertaining to Great Whites found in other parts of the world.

In this book, we not only provide coverage of Great White Shark biology, ecology and behaviour, but we also tackle conservation topics and the issue of cage diving, chumming and shark bites. We would like this book to serve as a resource for a wide audience, including cage-diving tourists, shark enthusiasts, naturalist guides and professional scientists, as well as swimmers, divers, spear fishermen, surfers and kayakers. We hope that already converted 'Great White junkies' will gain a better understanding of this shark's ecology, behaviour and conservation plight, while those that still fear the Great White will replace their fear with enthusiasm and insight.

Some readers might find it frustrating that, in places, we are unable to offer scientific certainties based on irrefutable evidence, and that we have had to resort to theories and hypotheses to explain some of our observations. However, to limit ourselves to scientific results that have weathered the test of time with a species as secretive and little studied as the Great White Shark would result in an incomplete book. As marine scientists, we have the responsibility to distinguish clearly between theory and fact, but it is also our task, where verifiable facts are sparse, to present the latest data, observations and theories, to examine them critically and to propose what we consider to be logical and valid conclusions, based on our experience.

Today, thanks largely to tourism, the Great White is worth more alive than dead. Seeing this animal in the flesh can make a person reconsider his or her preconceptions of the

Great White Sharks are usually more curious than aggressive. The shark in this image was about to give the dome port on the camera housing a gentle bump, most probably to investigate.

Great White as a wanton killer. This book, therefore, also aims to be a guide for those wishing to encounter the Great White in the flesh, not only covering the where, when and how of cage diving, but – more importantly – helping to select a knowledgeable, ethical and conservation-minded operator. Humans almost exterminated the species once, in the wake of the hysteria created by the film *JAWS*. We hope that now, in more enlightened times and despite the sensation created around shark bites on local shores, we will not make the same mistake again.

Over the years, we have had the privilege of spending thousands of days in the presence of these 'great' sharks. This book is our way of ensuring, in small part, some security of tenure to the Great White Shark, and of making the ocean a safer place for people and sharks alike.

Thomas P. Peschak & Michael C. Scholl

MARINE BIOLOGY RESEARCH INSTITUTE, UNIVERSITY OF CAPE TOWN

FACT FILE

- **Common names:** <u>English</u>: Great White Shark, Great White, White Shark, White Pointer; <u>Afrikaans</u>: *Withaai, Witdoodshaai*.
- **Family:** Lamnidae.
- **Scientific name:** *Carcharodon carcharias.*
- **Size:** Up to 6.1 m in length, weighing up to 1.9 tons. Males reach sexual maturity at between 3.5 and 4.1 m, and females at the much larger size of between 4 and 5 m.
- **Coloration:** Dorsal surface ranges from dark grey to light brown, while the ventral surface is white.
- **Range/Distribution:** Great Whites are widely distributed across southern Africa's oceans with the highest concentrations occurring in temperate waters, particularly in the vicinity of Cape fur seal colonies. They are also found in tropical and sub-tropical seas.
- **Reproduction:** Two to 10 embryos develop in the mother's uterus, each nourished by a yolk sac; when this supply is depleted, they feed on unfertilised eggs. The female gives birth to live young between 1.1 and 1.65 m in length after a gestation period of around 14 to 18 months.
- **Body temperature:** Its counter-current heat exchange system enables the Great White to keep vital organs up to 14°C warmer than the surrounding water.
- **Swimming speed:** Up to nearly 50 km per hour in short bursts. During ocean crossings, a minimum sustained speed of 4.7 km per hour.
- **Teeth:** 26 broad triangular-shaped and serrated teeth in each row of the upper jaw and 24 more pointed teeth in the lower jaw rows.
- **Prey:** Cape fur seals, other sharks, rays, bony fishes, dolphins, whales.
- **Main threats:** Commercial long lining; poaching for jaws, teeth and fins; KwaZulu-Natal shark nets; trawler and purse seiner by-catch; entanglement in and persecution from aquaculture facilities; boat traffic.

1 ORIGINS AND EVOLUTION

Sharks have roamed our oceans for more than 400 million years, which is at least 200 million years earlier than the dinosaurs and 396 million years before the evolution of the first hominids. Unfortunately, the shark's skeleton of cartilage preserves very poorly, unlike bone, so complete shark fossils are very rare and often the only relics that remain to piece together the morphology and natural history of early sharks are a mix of tiny scales and teeth. From as far back as 330 million years ago, the shark fauna began to diversify and proliferate in the oceans to such an extent that these fish came to occupy almost every niche. The sharks' ancient lineage, however, does not equate them with primitive creatures or – as they are sometimes referred to – living fossils. In fact, this group of fish has never stopped evolving and adapting to an ever-changing world.

The sharks of the early prehistoric days (330 million years ago) looked outlandish and bizarre, some with circular spiral jaws and others with a brush-like structure perched on top of their head. The first of what could be called 'modern' sharks evolved about 200 million years ago at the beginning of a geological period known today as the Jurassic, which was also the heyday of the dinosaurs. The sharks that shared the planet with Tyrannosaurus Rex and Brontosaurus would have been very familiar to us; they were streamlined, had two dorsal fins, a powerful vertical tail and a flexible jaw that could be thrust forward to feed. In fact, most of the shark families that are still around today evolved during this period, as

Evolutionary controversy

Currently, there are two conflicting theories on how Great White Sharks evolved and we will examine both of them. Is today's biggest carnivorous fish descended from the massive Megalodon, or does it relate more closely to the ancient mako shark look-alike, *Isurus hastalis*?

Heir of the monstrous Megalodon

Many people will have heard of Megalodon: the largest predatory shark that ever lived and probably the most formidable our world has ever seen. Megalodon reached lengths of perhaps over 15 m and weighed up to 50 tons (the approximate weight of 10 fully grown elephants). The gape of its mouth is said to have exceeded 2 m and its teeth reached almost 20 cm in length. The species is likely to have roamed prehistoric oceans from 20 million years ago and is believed to have become extinct only as recently as 2 million years ago, although the reasons for its demise are still not known. It is believed that Megalodon hunted and scavenged large whales. Around the time of its disappearance, many baleen whale species had begun migrating seasonally into the Arctic and Antarctic oceans to feed, possibly leaving Megalodon unable to follow its prey into such icy waters, a limitation that would have triggered its decline.

Megalodon (left) and Great White Shark (right) teeth.

Some scientists believe that the modern-day Great White Shark is descended from the same evolutionary branch that spawned Megalodon and have, therefore, placed the two species in the same genus – *Carcharodon* – based largely on the fact that both species have distinctly serrated teeth.

Descendant of the long-extinct *Isurus*

Another camp of shark palaeontologists believes, instead, that Megalodon was an evolutionary dead-end and that the Great White Shark evolved from the long-extinct *Isurus hastalis*, a species resembling present-day mako sharks. The teeth of *Isurus* and the modern-day Great Whites are remarkably similar in shape, differing only in that the former lack the characteristic serrations of the latter. However, several specimens of 23-million-year-old fossilised shark teeth similar to those of *Isurus*, but with weak serrations, have been found, possibly indicating the presence of a transitional form, and making it more likely that the Great White Shark descended from *Isurus*. The proponents of the *Isurus* theory, therefore, place Megalodon in a different genus from the Great White: *Carcharocles* and not *Carcharodon*.

Regardless of which evolutionary route proves to be correct, it is clear that while today, *Carcharodon carcharias* is the only living species of Great White Shark, the discovery of further fossilised teeth indicates that, around 20 million years ago, at least four other Great White species roamed the oceans. Through a taxonomic blunder as recently as in the 1800s, the presence of two different species of Great White was suspected: Dr Andrew Smith of the British Museum suggested that a two-metre-long Great White captured off the coast of the Cape was, in fact, a different species, and named it *Carcharodon capensis*. Thus, for a few short years, South Africa was able to claim its very own species of shark. Soon, however, the notion of a modern-day South African endemic was dispelled as other scientists examined the specimen and discovered that it was not a different species after all.

An unmistakable calling card: the distinctive dorsal fin of a Great White Shark slices through the water at dusk near Dyer Island.

2 THE GREAT GREAT WHITE

The biblical story reads: 'Now the Lord had prepared a great fish to swallow up Jonah, and he was in the belly of the fish for three days and three nights'. The same text passage in Greek refers to the animal as a sea monster (*ketos*). The 'fish' or 'sea monster' in this story is generally taken to be a whale. However, a baleen whale would not have been able to swallow a human – its funnel-shaped throat is extremely narrow (less than 10 cm in diameter), and designed to swallow mostly tiny krill. The only whale, in theory, large enough to swallow a human would be the sperm whale; this toothed whale, however, is only very rarely encountered in the Mediterranean Sea, where the incident is said to have taken place. It is therefore possible that this passage could hold the earliest

Size, form and function

The Great White Shark's formidable size has been the subject of endless controversy and, when assessing the species' maximum length, imaginations have been known to run wild. In the book *South African Beachcomber*, author Lawrence Green recounts the onslaught of that deadly illness, the plague, on a boat anchored in False Bay in the days of sailing vessels. The boat was refused entry into port for fear of contagion, and the sailors were forced to carry out many sea burials. According to this account, Great White Sharks in excess of 13 m in length were seen feeding on the dead. Tall tales of Great Whites the size of dinosaurs are not restricted to the annals of history. Even today, it is claimed that a Great White in excess of 8 m, nicknamed 'The Submarine', haunts False Bay near Cape Town. However, as with Green's monster sharks several centuries ago, no verifiable records have ever been obtained.

The jaws of a 5.9-metre Great White Shark caught off Danger Point dwarf the shark researcher holding the massive structure.

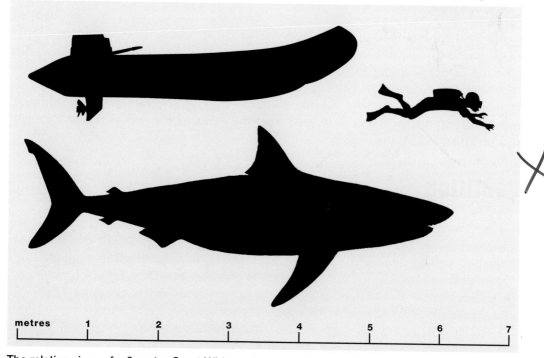

metres   1   2   3   4   5   6   7

The relative sizes of a 6-metre Great White, a 4-metre inflatable boat and a 2-metre diver.

Great Whites do grow to epic proportions in both length and girth, but none on record has been known to exceed 7 m. In fact, the world's largest accurately measured specimen was 6.1 m long and caught in August 1983 at Prince Edward Island off the Canadian Atlantic coast. In South Africa the largest shark ever landed was 5.9 m, caught off Danger Point near Gansbaai. The girth of a mature adult is every bit as impressive as its length, and an underwater meeting with a fully mature individual can be likened to encountering a small bus. Unlike a bus, however, and despite a weight of up to 1.9 tons, Great Whites possess the ability to move and turn with lightning speed because, like all sharks, their skeletons are cartilage instead of bone. This represents several advantages for the shark: not only is cartilage more flexible, but it is also significantly lighter than a comparative bony skeleton would be, allowing the shark to move with greater speed. Cartilage is also not as dense as bone and, because Great White Sharks lack a swim bladder (an air-filled structure in many fishes that allows them to maintain buoyancy) the cartilaginous skeleton helps achieve some degree of neutral buoyancy when swimming.

A Great White Shark's body is covered from head to tail by placoid scales or dermal denticles, an assemblage of minuscule scales or 'teeth'. By virtue of their strength, design and arrangement, these scales afford the shark two important advantages. First, they act as armour, protecting the fish from major injuries; and secondly, they minimise friction the shark would encounter when swimming. As water passes over the shark's skin, it forms a film between the denticles, reducing turbulence and allowing the shark to glide in a near-frictionless manner. The combination of a cartilaginous skeleton, tooth-like dermal denticles, powerful swim muscles and torpedo-shaped body enable the Great White Shark to reach (over a short distance) a speed of close to 50 km per hour, making it one of the fastest fish in the ocean.

Speed and mobility are essential, too, for the Great White Shark's breathing. Unlike shark species that spend much of their time on or near the seabed, the Great White does not have the ability to ventilate its gills by pumping water through them while immobile. The Great White has to swim constantly, mouth ajar, in order to breathe. As it swims, water flows into the mouth and passes through the gills, where hundreds of fine, feathered filaments absorb oxygen from the water, before it exits through five gill slits on either side of the head.

Dentition

In 1785 Carolus Linnaeus classified the Great White in his catalogue *Systema Naturae* as *Squalus carcharias*. Only 100 years later did it become known scientifically as *Carcharodon carcharias* – or 'jagged tooth' in Greek – a direct homage to its formidable dentition.

The 'smile' of the Great White is punctuated by 26 broad, triangular, serrated teeth in each row of the upper jaw and 24 teeth in the lower jaw rows. The lower teeth are more slender and pointed, designed to impale, while the upper teeth have evolved to cut and saw.

Great Whites, as with all shark species, have many rows of teeth, with only the first few being functional at any one time. Teeth fall out or break regularly and are replaced automatically throughout the shark's life.

The teeth in a Great White's lower jaw are designed to impale and are more slender and pointed than the broader-shaped cutting teeth of the upper jaw.

Camouflage

While its teeth may have inspired its scientific name, the common name is clearly based on the shark's appearance. It remains a mystery, however, why this shark is referred to as 'white' when such coloration is restricted to the ventral (lower) surface of the shark's body. The coloration of the dorsal (upper) surface ranges from dark grey to light brown. This

Gustation (taste) organs are located in the shark's mouth and throat, and are used primarily to help the shark decide whether something is edible or not. When a shark bites a potential food item, clusters of microscopic taste buds in its mouth are activated, informing the shark of the taste, and possibly even the calorific value. A bad-tasting or low-calorie item, such as a human or seabird, is spat out, while palatable, energy-rich prey, such as a seal, is consumed.

A Great White Shark's sense of smell is extremely acute, and up to 18 per cent of its brain mass is used to analyse information picked up by the olfactory bulbs in the nasal cavities.

Hearing

A Great White's hearing system is very different from our own three-part ear system. The shark has only an inner ear and all sound vibrations pass directly through the shark's skin and tissue from the surrounding water. A Great White can also sense and pinpoint the origin of vibrations with another organ, its 'lateral line' system. This is a series of sensory pores along the head and sides of all sharks, by which water currents, vibrations, and pressure changes are detected. Water displacement creates a series of weak pressure ripples that sharks are able to detect. An injured or sick fish would swim more clumsily (and would create much stronger pulses) than a fish swimming normally and creating little turbulence. These irregular pulses would trigger the shark's lateral line receptors from much further away than would the regular, more muted pulses produced by a healthy fish.

Vision

In spite of their other highly developed sensory systems, Great Whites rely mostly on their sense of sight for hunting. They possess two types of retina cells: rods, adapted to detect contrast and movement even at low light levels, and cones, specialised to discern detail and different colours in conditions of higher light levels. The rod-to-cone ratio in the Great White's retina is about 4:1 (similar to that of the human eye), allowing for precise colour vision – and refuting claims that all sharks have poor vision. Moreover, sharks' eyes have a remarkable feature, the *tapetum lucidum,* which is similar to that of the eyes of cats and other nocturnal animals. Located just behind the retina, this structure comprises an arrangement of miniature plates layered with the silvery substance guanine. Rays of light streaming into the eye hit the shark's retina and then are reflected off these 'mirrors' to pass through the retina a second time, doubling its photosensitivity in low light conditions. Conversely, in order to protect their eyesight in bright daylight, Great White Sharks also have migratory pigment cells that can obstruct the plates to prevent light from hitting the sensory cells a second time. The result is similar to the effect produced by photochromic sunglasses, which darken in bright light. Most shark species have a protective nictitating membrane to protect their eyes, similar to our eyelids. Great Whites, however, lack this membrane, and instead roll their eyes backwards in their sockets to protect them when approaching unknown objects or striking prey. Contrary to the popular idea that Great Whites have 'dead' black eyes, the iris is actually a very deep blue, clearly visible in bright sunlight (see opposite).

A sixth sense

Great Whites, like all sharks, possess a 'sixth' sense that humans lack: 'electroreception'. Multiple rows of tiny pores are positioned mainly on the snout and head of the shark. These pores lead into small interlinked cavities, known as the *ampullae of Lorenzini,* filled with an electrically conductive jelly. These ampullae enable sharks to detect the electrical currents created by muscular tissue activity in living creatures, and to locate prey even in the absence of vision at night or in murky conditions. Great Whites rely on this sense during the final stages of a hunt, when they roll their eyes backwards in their sockets to protect them from injury.

Electroreception is also used by some shark species to navigate, and enables them to sense the Earth's magnetic field, and orient themselves during ocean crossings or in the absence of other geographical landmarks.

A Great White Shark's vision is believed to be as good above as under water. Sharks frequently raise their head out of the water near busy cage-diving boats to investigate the activity.

Great Whites have one of the widest habitat and geographic ranges of any fish. The species' ability to regulate body temperature enables it to inhabit all of our planet's oceans – from the cold seas to the tropics and from coastal to oceanic realms. It is important to note that, to date, no Great White has been shown to remain long in any particular area, and it is much more likely that these sharks are only short-term inhabitants of any given region, being constantly on the move. This said, the highest concentrations of Great Whites are found in temperate seas, especially in the vicinity of seal islands and offshore banks rich in fish resources.

South Africa's best known Great White hot spots all lie off the shores of the Western Cape: Seal Island in Mossel Bay, Dyer Island and Geyser Rock near Gansbaai and Seal Island in False Bay near Cape Town (see Chapters 3 and 4). These permanent seal colonies act as magnets for Great Whites on their journey along the coastline, and represent ideal temporary feeding grounds. Great Whites also occur in significant numbers off the KwaZulu-Natal coast and have been recorded off Namibia, possibly even from the coast of Angola, but reliable information from that locality is in short supply.

The highest concentrations of Great White Sharks in Africa occur in South Africa's temperate seas off the Western Cape coast. Kelp forests and rocky reefs characterise the marine

There are many records of Great White sightings and catches in the western Indian Ocean. A few sightings in Mozambican waters by scuba divers and the tracking of a satellite-tagged shark from Mossel Bay in South Africa to Mozambique indicate that these sharks could be more common along that tropical coastline than previously believed. In Kenya, at least two Great Whites have been caught by fishermen off the coast of Malindi: a 5-m male (1989) and a 6.4-m pregnant female (1996). In Zanzibar, 35 km off the coast of Tanzania, local fishermen reportedly catch one or two Great Whites annually. These sharks also occur off the coasts of the Mascarene Islands: in 1971, a shark of nearly 5 m was caught off Mauritius, while in 2003, one of 3–3.5 m was spotted by a scuba diver at that same locality. Two Great White Sharks were also caught off the coast of neighbouring Reunion. However, most Great White records from the western Indian Ocean come from the island of Madagascar, where 17 catches were recorded between 1994 and 2001.

In southern Africa, reports of Great White Sharks have been received from Namibia, South Africa and Mozambique, and they possibly also occur in Angolan waters.

Great White Sharks also inhabit warmer tropical seas and have been sighted and recorded from the coral reefs of Kenya and Tanzania, as well as from the reefs of Indian Ocean Islands such as Madagascar and Mauritius.

3 SUPREME PREDATOR

The Great White Shark's impressive collection of traits discussed in Chapter 2, finely tuned over millions of years of evolution, enable it to remain at the top of the food chain in most of the world's oceans. Only where killer whales are abundant does the Great White encounter a rival and, even then, the two species stay well clear of one another most of the time. There is an isolated report of two killer whales attacking and killing a Great White off the North American West Coast. Killer whales, however, are rare in southern African waters where the Great White rules supreme.

Studying Great White Shark diet

Studying the diet and feeding behaviour of a large and potentially dangerous marine predator is not an easy task. In the early days of international shark research, investigating the diet of Great Whites was limited to cataloguing the stomach contents of sharks caught and killed by the researchers themselves. In South Africa, however, Great Whites were not systematically pursued for science, and even during the heyday of trophy fishing, little attention was paid to stomach contents. Only when shark nets (aimed at catching sharks to decrease their population and reduce the incidents of shark bites) were installed off the coast of KwaZulu-Natal in the 1960s was a steady supply of dead Great White Sharks available for research purposes. Owing to this development, South African scientists were able to study between 20 and 60 specimens a year. Extensive research on stomach contents reveals that Great White Sharks caught in the shark nets preferentially feed on other sharks and rays, with juvenile dusky sharks being the most common prey item in their diet. Bony fishes come a close second: sardines feature prominently during the sardine run in June/July; species such as cob and sea bream dominate at other times of the year. Marine mammals rank third, with the remains of bottlenose and common dolphins and whales evident. It is well to bear in mind, however, that the shark-net data does not present the complete picture of the Great White Shark's dietary ecology in South Africa and that all results relate only to sharks caught in shark nets off the subtropical KwaZulu-Natal coast.

While Great Whites will bite non-food items, they are highly specialised hunters and are very selective in what they actually eat.

One finding from the shark-net data, however, has more wide-ranging implications. In stark contrast to tiger sharks, which have been nicknamed 'the garbage cans of the oceans' because of their indiscriminate feeding behaviour (their stomach contents have been known to include boat cushions, clothing, nuts and bolts, license plates and even an unopened tin of salmon), indigestible non-food items are largely lacking from Great Whites' stomachs. This significant absence indicates that the Great White Shark is not an indiscriminate predator that will devour anything in its path: it is a selective and highly specialised hunter.

Prey of the Great White Shark

The diet of the Great White Shark in South African waters is more diverse than previously believed and, in addition to feeding on other sharks, rays, bony fish and cetaceans, as stomach-contents research shows, Cape fur seals are also a prominent prey item.

Cape fur seals

Cape fur seals constitute an important food source for sharks along the southern African coast, except in the waters off KwaZulu-Natal and those of the northern reaches of the Eastern Cape, where seal colonies are conspicuously absent. The highest concentrations of Great Whites are found in the vicinity of such colonies and, in order to study how sharks hunt seals, scientists rely largely on behavioural observations made from research boats in the vicinity of these 'hot spots'.

Although Great Whites target seals from most of South Africa's major seal colonies, the spectacular breaching predations that occur at Seal Island in False Bay have garnered most of the scientific attention (see pages 29–32). Alternative research observation points such as Dyer Island (near Gansbaai) have yielded far fewer and less spectacular hunts that only rarely involve high breaches – for reasons not yet understood. Many kills at these latter venues appear to happen sub-surface, and often the only indication that a successful hunt has taken place is the flocks of gulls scavenging on the shark's leftovers. Anecdotal accounts suggest that the number of seal predations was significantly higher at Dyer Island before the inception of large-scale shark tourism, and today's boom in ecotourism clearly makes for crowded research conditions.

Cape fur seals, an important prey item for Great White Sharks off southern Africa's temperate coasts, breed at numerous island locations. When the pups are six to seven months old, they start swimming out to feed, at which time the highest concentrations of sharks are recorded.

ON THE HUNT AT SEAL ISLAND

The annual arrival of large numbers of Great White Sharks at Seal Island in March/April coincides with the time when Cape fur seal pups (born in November/December of the previous year) begin to spend prolonged periods of time in the water, supplementing their milk diet with prey caught in the vicinity of the colony. When the pups are seven months of age, in June/July, they begin to forage at considerable distances from the colony, and this correlates well with peak Great White Shark concentrations at the island.

Cape fur seals, both adults and the more advanced of the year's pups, leave the island to feed in groups of up to 50 individuals. This behaviour is so ingrained that often large numbers will wait in the shallows, in the so-called 'launch pad' area, until enough have assembled to swim out in one large 'body'. This strategy allows for many more pairs of eyes to keep a lookout for Great Whites, and also makes it much harder for the shark to single out one individual target. Once out at sea, however, the seals disperse to feed and, consequently, often return alone or in much smaller groups. A lone seal is a much easier target and it is for this reason that the bulk of attacks occur when they are returning to shore.

The chase

The physiologies of Cape fur seals and Great White Sharks are very different. Great Whites are capable of extremely rapid bursts of speed, but do not have the stamina of their preferred prey. Cape fur seals are almost as quick as Great Whites, but are considerably better in terms of endurance. In order to capture a seal, therefore, the shark needs the element of

Most predations at Seal Island occur in the early hours of the morning, especially right before dawn, when little light penetrates the water. Even once the sun has come up, the day's first rays of light hit the ocean's surface at such a steep angle that little of it actually enters the water. Great Whites swim along the seabed, scanning the surface of the water for the distinct silhouettes of seals; even in low-light conditions, seals are clearly visible against the very bright surface. Conversely, sharks are unlikely to be detected by seals because their dark dorsal surface blends perfectly with the seabed. Once a seal has been spotted, the shark initiates the chase.

This may take a variety of forms, depending on the angle from which the shark approaches its prey. A steep, vertical ascent will result in the shark's leaping completely out of the water (see page 29), sometimes even tipping right over so that it re-enters the water head first. If the angle of attack is less steep, then the shark will breach in a more horizontal fashion (see opposite) and enter the water with a 'belly flop'. If the shark does not catch the seal on the first attempt, it instantly loses the vital element of surprise and the odds quickly swing in favour of the seal. The seal employs an array of evasive manoeuvres to stay away from the shark's mouth by leaping and zigzagging in an effort to get behind its attacker. The seal has nothing to lose and will expend every last ounce of energy to escape. The shark, on the other hand, must ensure that the energy it expends in pursuit is less than the prey is worth in terms of energy

BELOW: Leaving the island in large groups, seals will 'porpoise' from the water as a defence against Great Whites on the hunt. OPPOSITE: In pursuit of Cape fur seals, the Great Whites that frequent False Bay's Seal Island during the winter months will often leap from the water.

gain. If the seal manages to evade the shark's jaws for long enough, the shark will give up the chase because of the disproportionate amount of energy required to sustain it.

Most successful attacks are swift and, from first strike to total consumption, last less than a minute. Compared to most terrestrial predators, the Great White's success rate is remarkably high and about 50 per cent of all observed attacks end in successful predation. Lions and tigers, by contrast, are successful in 30 per cent of their hunts and only the cheetah, the most successful cat predator, outclasses the Great White with a 70 per cent success rate.

Cape fur seals are not as defenceless against Great White Sharks as they might seem. A 4-m Great White was observed approaching a small seal colony on the Robberg Peninsula near Plettenberg Bay when a large adult bull seal responded by repeatedly charging at the shark, finally chasing it away from the area. There are also reports of large pods of seals chasing Great Whites out of Shark Alley, between Dyer Island and Geyser Rock in False Bay when the water is clear.

Drawn invariably to every kill, flocks of seagulls rapidly appear and devour any left-over scraps.

Fish

While seals certainly are an important part of their diet, Great Whites off South Africa's temperate coast will, like their counterparts off the KwaZulu-Natal coast, also consume large numbers of other sharks and bony fish. However, since only a handful of Great Whites' stomachs have been examined from outside the KwaZulu-Natal region, it is impossible to put a figure on what percentage of their diet comprises seals as opposed to fish. Great Whites are often observed in areas where large concentrations of game fish abound and are known to steal struggling fish from spear fishermen; they will also readily take yellowtail from the hooks of line fishermen.

A possible explanation for the varied diet of Great Whites, which includes both seals and fish, is that their preferences change as they mature. This is supported by an examination of Great Whites' jaws, which reveal that, as the animal matures, the teeth progressively change from narrow, stabbing teeth to broader, cutting teeth. Furthermore, in regions where more substantial stomach content data has been gathered, it has been found that smaller sharks have a dietary preference for fish but, as they grow larger and their dentition changes, their diet shifts towards marine mammals.

Dolphins

It is clear from direct observation that Great Whites hunt seals, but the fact that they also eat dolphins derives largely from indirect evidence, such as the stomach contents of sharks caught in shark nets. But this does not provide conclusive proof that Great Whites actually *hunt* bottlenose and common dolphins, as these two species regularly fall prey to shark nets, and could have been *scavenged* as opposed to preyed upon. However, many dolphins are observed out at sea with extensive scarring and, while it is not possible to identify what species of shark caused these injuries, the size and shape of the residual scars does not exclude – and perhaps even favours – the Great White.

The remains of both bottlenose (front) and hump-backed (behind) dolphins have been found in the stomachs of Great Whites, but whether they have been hunted or scavenged is still under debate among researchers.

Great Whites and hump-backed dolphins frequently swim close to one another off the Cape coast. These dolphins are more agile and quicker than the sharks and it is possible that, as with seals, the Great White has to use stealth and surprise to hunt hump-backed dolphins successfully. The shark's ambush tactics could include concealing itself in murky water. The behaviour of some hump-backed dolphins may, in part, confirm this, as they appear to avoid murky water and head offshore at night, possibly to avoid encountering sharks when conditions are not in their favour. It is also likely that sharks prefer to target old, young, or sick and injured animals.

Whales

There is plenty of evidence to suggest that Great White Sharks regularly consume whale meat, although the likelihood that they would hunt or kill large whales is very slight: a Great White is no match for an adult whale and even a young one can give a Great White a run for its money.

However, from time to time whale carcasses drift past Seal or Dyer Islands – the animals having been killed by ship collisions or entanglement – and make for a Great White banquet. The whales offer the Great Whites a convenient and plentiful meal, high in energy-rich blubber. The shark's metabolism is generally slow and the ability to stock up reserves in its huge fatty liver allows it to go without feeding for several weeks. If a windfall like a dead whale comes along, sharks will eat their fill in anticipation of lean times ahead.

These banquets have revealed another aspect of Great White behaviour: it appears that, at such feasts, they adopt temporary social rankings based on size and dominance. Sometimes up to 30 Great Whites feed together, queuing in an almost orderly fashion to feed.

Seabirds

There are many records of Great White Sharks biting seabirds, and African penguins in particular, off the South African coast. However, there is only a single record of a bird – a penguin – found in a Great White's stomach. A comprehensive study of scars

and injuries to penguins on Bird Island, off Port Elizabeth on the east coast, showed that many had been bitten by Great Whites. Cape gannets in the area also exhibit such injuries. The fact that so many penguins commonly survive Great White bites suggests that the injuries sustained were not because they were *hunted* – a full feeding bite would kill. Unlike seals or cetaceans (whales and dolphins), which are composed largely of fatty blubber, seabirds consist mainly of muscle, with too low an energy content to be considered a worthy prey item. (In a similar way, Californian sea otters regularly wash up on the beaches of California with Great White bite marks.) African penguins may be mistaken for suitable prey and then rejected owing to their low nutritional value, or they may be used as target practice by juvenile sharks; or perhaps they are unknowing pawns in Great White play behaviour. Since these birds have evolved side by side with Great Whites for millions of years, it is unlikely that so many sharks mistake penguins for profitable prey. The play-and-practice hunting theory would appear to have more merit.

LEFT: African penguins are often the victims of inquisitive sharks' bites. *OPPOSITE:* When a whale carcass drifts past a Great White hot spot like Dyer Island, the sharks feast on the rich blubber until there is nothing left, or until the carcass is beached on the shore.

4 GREAT WHITES INSHORE

One morning while out on our research boat in what is now known as Shark Bay – an inshore area just ten kilometres to the north of the renowned Dyer Island and Shark Alley – a scene greeted us that could have been spliced straight from the film *JAWS*. Close to a sandy beach, which was packed with swimmers and sun-worshippers, we spotted a dark shape cruising in the shallows. We quickly moved inshore to investigate and watched as the creature inadvertently revealed its identity while passing over a sandbar: a large, steely-grey, triangular dorsal fin punctured the glassy surface, and what was unmistakably a Great White Shark headed into water so shallow that whirlwinds of sand followed in its wake.

Interpreting the habits of sharks

Most people, on seeing a shark in such proximity to a bathing beach would assume it to be *en route* to finding itself a mid-morning snack. But this Great White was focused on its own, private mission and swam straight past bathers splashing in the surf. The very next day we encountered three more Great Whites within 50 m of the beach, and a further five after cruising in an easterly direction. We commenced daily inshore surveys, and quickly realised that our first encounters were no fluke, and that large numbers of Great White Sharks were congregating in the shallow waters. On some of our six nautical-mile-long transects, we encountered more than 20 individual White Sharks, an astonishing statistic – over three sharks per mile of beach.

We had known for some years that, in summer, Great Whites frequent the deeper reaches of Shark Bay. What we did not know was that they travel this close inshore, and in such great numbers. Every dawn of that first inshore research season delivered new surprises until, one day in January, the shark encounters suddenly stopped. For weeks we continued with the surveys, but the sharks had gone. Soon the Great Whites also disappeared from the deeper reaches of the bay, and we moved our research offshore to Dyer Island, a familiar research site and 'home' to what is possibly the world's highest concentration of transient Great Whites.

FINPRINTING

In the early days of Great White research in South Africa, sharks were tagged with numbered or colour-coded tags. However, this method of identifying individual sharks was inadequate and largely unsuccessful as the tags were subject to profuse algae growth that quickly made them illegible and predisposed them to falling off. Another method of identifying sharks for follow-up research was required.

Cetacean biologists had known for decades that the dorsal fins of dolphins, and the tail flukes of some whales, present a host of very obvious markings that can be used to identify individual specimens in much the same way that human individuals can be identified by their fingerprints. In the 1990s, it was proposed that the unique markings on the dorsal fins of Great White Sharks could be used in the same way to identify individual sharks. After considerable research, sufficient proof was gathered to show that Great Whites could indeed be reliably identified using each individual specimen's unique trailing edge notch pattern, shape of the tip and pigmentation patches that are sometimes present on the dorsal fin. This technique, named finprinting, presents several advantages in that it is non-invasive and can be performed at a distance. It has allowed over 1 000 Great Whites to be identified at Dyer Island since 1997, and, consequently, the regularity of their visits to be tracked.

A Great White Shark's dorsal fin is as good as a human fingerprint for identification, with the serrated pattern along the trailing edge being unique to each shark.

Inshore or offshore?

There is a distinct seasonal component to the presence and absence of Great White Sharks off South Africa's temperate southwest coast. Between September and late January, Great Whites frequent the deeper reaches of Shark Bay close to the mainland and, from October onwards, they also venture into the very shallow near-shore waters. Between March and September, shark numbers are highest around offshore Dyer Island. Where the majority of Great Whites retreat to during February and March is not yet known, as the number of sharks encountered both inshore and offshore is very low. Evidence for similar seasonal patterns is also emerging for other locations. Great Whites are most abundant around False Bay's Seal Island from May to September, and also move inshore during the summer months. Seal Island at Mossel Bay, which is situated just a few hundred metres from the mainland, has seasonal patterns that are much less distinct.

Population data collected at Dyer Island and in Shark Bay, such as length and gender, shows that the sharks at these two locations are very different from one another. More than 95 per cent of Great Whites encountered in Shark Bay are females, while the population around Dyer Island has a more balanced makeup of 60 per cent females and 40 per cent males. The sharks inshore also comprise a combination of extreme sizes of shark, both distinctly larger (over 4 m) and considerably smaller individuals (less than 2.5 m), but very few sizes in between. At Dyer Island, most of the sharks are in the 3.5 m range. In addition, female sharks in Shark Bay exhibit high frequencies of fresh bite wounds and scars around the pectoral fins and gill area.

It appears that Great Whites don't visit the shallows of Shark Bay to hunt, as those individuals we have tracked ignored the chum slicks of cage-diving boats.

Theories and hypotheses

Taking all of this evidence into account, we constructed three hypotheses as to why Great White Sharks were congregating so close to the shore.

Hunting theory

We first thought that the sharks were assembling around a seasonally abundant food source, and systematically searched the shallows for signs of potential prey species. While we encountered runs of game fish and some seals in the deeper reaches of the bay, much of the immediate inshore area, bar a few stingrays, was barren, resembling an undersea desert. The sharks we tracked also ignored the chum slicks of cage-diving boats pushed inshore by wind and currents, swimming straight through them without bothering to investigate or respond to them. This is in stark contrast to shark behaviour in the deeper reaches of the bay, where they are readily attracted to cage-diving boats with chum, and attempt to feed on the bait. The evidence suggested that they were not coming inshore to hunt.

Pupping theory

In some species of shark, feeding inhibition occurs during pregnancy and immediately after giving birth, to prevent newly born sharks from falling prey to their own mothers. A White Shark birth has never been observed, but the smallest sharks spotted inshore fitted within the estimated size of newly-born sharks, between 1.2 and 1.5 m. Many species of shark make use of shallow bays to give birth and to allow their young to mature, and we began thinking that perhaps we had discovered a pupping ground. However, this theory would not explain the higher incidence of fresh scars on female sharks in the inshore regions.

Mating theory

If Great White Sharks mate like most other species (mating has also never been observed), then biting and holding the female around her pectoral and dorsal fins by the male, in order to insert his claspers, could account for the observed scarring. In addition, while

The inshore region of Shark Bay resembles an undersea desert and, bar a few rays and the occasional pod of hump-backed dolphins that passes through, there seems little here for Great White Sharks to eat.

science has yet to prove this, we believe that Great White Sharks could also be inhibited from feeding while they are mating. Shark mating is a rough affair, and feeding inhibition, especially in males, would prevent potentially fatal injuries in a species as large and powerful as the Great White. During mating, the pair are obliged to stop swimming, and consequently sink. When this happens, and water no longer passes rapidly over their gills,

they become starved of oxygen. There could thus be two possible advantages to mating in shallow water: firstly, the sharks would be immersed in (or be very close to) the turbulent, oxygen-rich surf zone, allowing them to recover from mating-induced oxygen starvation more rapidly; and secondly, instead of sinking and possibly crashing to the rocky seabed, they would land gently on sand.

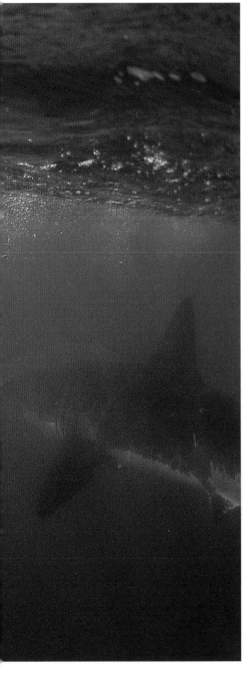

Research results

We do not believe that hunting generally lures sharks into the shallows of the bay, but that pupping or mating, or both, are more likely reasons. Still armed with more questions than answers, we need direct behavioural observations to supplement our indirect evidence. Using sea kayaks as our tracking platforms (see pages 44–45), we have documented high levels of social interaction inshore for what has always been considered a largely solitary species. The sharks methodically swim up and down parallel to the beach, their paths crossing at frequencies that are unlikely to be just random. We have observed that when two sharks meet, they swim ever-tighter circles around one another and then often follow each other along the beach over considerable distances. All social interactions noted have occurred at a slow and relaxed pace, without any of the sharks displaying signs of aggression or obvious competition. After three inshore research seasons, we have yet to observe either mating or pupping, and it will take more field time to establish, with any degree of certainty, what the sharks are doing there.

In the coming year, we will also add a further weapon to our inshore research arsenal: a tethered blimp equipped with a remote-controlled digital video camera that will beam down live images of a large section of False Bay for 10 hours every day. If any reproduction behaviour occurs in the shallows, we will not only be able to view it in real time, but also be able to record and analyse it in great detail.

During the summer months, social behaviour between Great White Sharks that could be related to mating is frequently observed, often involving swimming tight circles around, or following, one another.

KAYAKING WITH GREAT WHITES

Our motorised research vessel was of limited use in our study of inshore Great White Sharks: not only were we unable to enter very shallow water, but the electromagnetic discharges and vibrations emitted by the engines disrupt sharks' natural behaviour. They were either persistently attracted to, or repelled from, the boat. We chose a non-motorised mode of transport that was manoeuvrable and, more importantly, quiet – sea kayaks. Even though experience had taught us that words such as 'cautious' and 'inquisitive' describe the Great White Shark's character much more accurately than 'aggressive' or 'unpredictable', we still felt vulnerable with only a few centimetres of yellow plastic sea kayak separating us from them. Upon first encountering the kayaks, the sharks circled us cautiously; but they soon became comfortable enough to swim alongside us to within a metre of our vessels. As we had hoped, they then continued on their way, disregarding our presence completely, allowing us to track them discreetly and observe their natural behaviour.

Looming menace – or peaceful visitor?

Shark Bay's remote beaches, of which only a few hundred metres out of 7 km are used for swimming and surfing, is not the only spot where Great Whites move inshore during the summer months. Both False Bay and the western shores of the Cape Peninsula also appear to harbour seasonally high concentrations of Great Whites. False Bay, however, is fringed with dozens of popular swimming and surfing beaches. When newspapers published aerial photographs of large numbers of Great White Sharks very close to Cape Town's packed bathing beaches, it confirmed that what we were observing in Shark Bay was not a localised event, but a much wider-ranging phenomenon. The public initially responded to the notion

ABOVE & LEFT: Most of the Great Whites that frequent the extreme inshore regions of Shark Bay appear to be very relaxed, and there are few signs, if any, of competitive feeding interactions.

of Great Whites so close to shore with fear and apprehension, and there were calls for the authorities to deal with the shark 'problem'. Suggestions ranged from government-subsidised shark hunting, to swelling tourism coffers by bringing in wealthy overseas tourists to hunt Great Whites, to installing shark nets. However, if the inshore aggregations are, in fact, related to mating or pupping, then, instead of persecuting these sharks, we should be protecting them from all forms of disturbance to ensure the survival of the species.

Large-scale Great White Shark research projects are currently underway: in False Bay, research is led by Alison Kock from the University of Cape Town, and in Mossel Bay by Ryan Johnson from the University of Pretoria. We hope that their research, in conjunction with ours, will shed light on why these sharks are coming inshore. In April 2005, in a project funded by the Save Our Seas Foundation, acoustic monitoring equipment was deployed in key areas around False Bay, including off bathing beaches, to examine the movements of Great Whites in the bay. The monitors, which work much like supermarket checkout scanners, record all specially tagged Great Whites that swim close by, and store the information for later analysis.

Shark spotting

Despite the public's initial misgivings, the newfound knowledge that Great Whites frequently swim in close proximity to bathing and surfing beaches has led to a surprising conservation success story. At a workshop held in Cape Town in June 2005, attended by all of South Africa's shark experts, the presence of Great White Sharks inshore was discussed and debated. The participants reached consensus on policy, ruling out the installation of shark nets as a solution. Instead of approaching the situation in an aggressive and intrusive manner, more ecologically benign action was suggested to prevent further dramatic encounters between Great White Sharks and people.

The mountainous shoreline of the Cape Peninsula provides ideal vantage points from which to detect Great White Sharks that approach bathing beaches. A community-driven and -funded initiative saw people from previously disadvantaged communities employed to scan the ocean adjacent to Peninsula beaches for any signs of Great Whites swimming close to shore. Equipped with radios, the 'spotters' can raise the alarm at the beach below. A siren is sounded and a 'shark flag' raised to warn everyone in the water to return to the beach immediately. Although this system is by no means foolproof, the aim is prevention as opposed to unnecessary intervention. In this way, Great White Sharks are treated as equal players in our shared ecosystem, rather than problems that need to be eradicated. Today, the shark-spotter programme is funded by the City of Cape Town and the WWF Sanlam Marine Programme, and is soon to be rolled out at many more beaches across the Western Cape.

To prevent further inshore encounters between Great White Sharks and people, a shark-spotter programme was initiated. When eagle-eyed spotters such as Monwabisi (right) sight a Great White from their hillside vantage point, they sound the alarm. Beach patrollers like Patrick (above) then spring into action and raise the shark flag to alert everyone in the water to the danger.

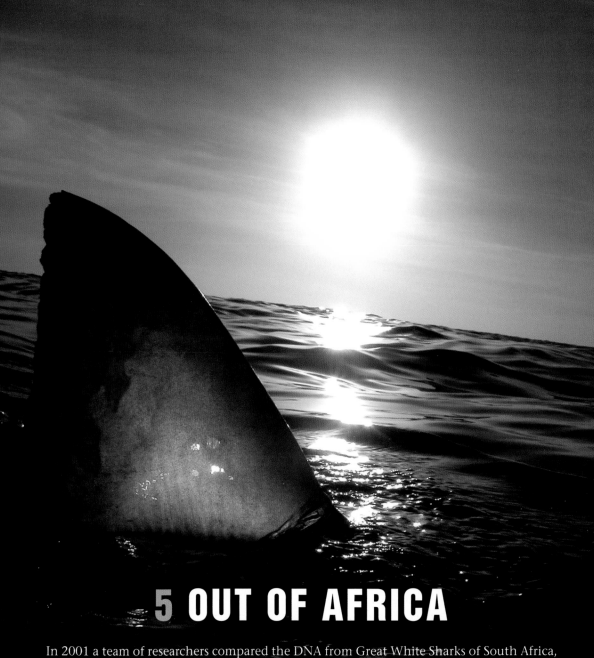

5 OUT OF AFRICA

In 2001 a team of researchers compared the DNA from Great White Sharks of South Africa, Australia and New Zealand and found that individuals from Australia and New Zealand were genetically different from South African sharks. This suggested that populations at opposite ends of the Indian Ocean are isolated from each other. Further genetic testing confirmed these results, with the exception of a 3.5-m male shark captured in Tasmania, which harboured genetic similarity to South African Great Whites. At the time, scientists postulated that males travel between Australia and South Africa, while females are bound to one continent. It was only four years later that part of this theory could be substantiated. In the end, however, it was a female shark, not a male, that brought us the first direct evidence of Great Whites crossing the Indian Ocean.

International protection of the Great White Shark

South Africa was the first country to declare the Great White Shark a protected species, but, although protected in South African waters since 1991, Great Whites are still under threat from local commercial fishing operations. Internationally they are also endangered, since most conservation agreements and conventions have little power to protect a species on a global scale. A notable exception is the Convention on International Trade in Endangered Species of Wild Fauna and Flora, more commonly known as CITES.

CITES is an international agreement between governments to ensure that the international trade in fauna and flora does not threaten the survival of individual species. Since its inception in 1963, not one species protected by CITES has become extinct as a result of trade.

In 2002, the Great White Shark was not listed on CITES, thus allowing trade in jaws, teeth and fins to flow freely across international borders. It had long been suspected that Great Whites themselves routinely crossed international maritime boundaries. In order to garner direct evidence of the migration of Great Whites across entire oceans, satellite tagging was essential. With a CITES meeting looming in 2004, scientists from the Wildlife Conservation Society and South African Marine and Coastal Management implemented an extensive satellite tagging project, with the aim of providing clear evidence that national protective measures were inadequate for a species like the Great White.

While protected in South African and Namibian waters, some Great White Sharks still die accidentally as a result of commercial fishing activities. The shark pictured here was mistakenly caught in a purse seine net near Mossel Bay in 2001, and subsequently died.

Gathering evidence

The first direct evidence that Great White Sharks leave South Africa's territorial waters was provided by a 2.8 m female, originally tagged off Mossel Bay with a SPOT satellite tag. She was tracked swimming along the eastern coastline of South Africa before heading several hundred kilometres offshore near Port St Johns. She then returned to the coast, this time off southern Mozambique where, unfortunately, the transmission from the satellite tag ceased.

Great Whites are not protected by conservation legislation along the coast of Mozambique, nor are they protected in international waters. While this journey into Mozambican waters was the first irrefutable evidence that Great White Sharks leave South Africa's protected seas, far more dramatic evidence was still to come, transmitted by the tracking device fitted to a female shark, named Nicole, in 2003.

TAGGING GREAT WHITES

Currently there are two main types of tags on the market: a SPOT or 'Smart Position Only Transmitter', which is attached to the dorsal fin of the shark and transmits a signal to an orbiting satellite every time the fin breaks the surface; and a PAT or 'Passive Archival Tag', which records and stores all the information on position, depth and water temperature until the tag detaches itself from the shark at a predetermined date, floats to the surface and sends the stored data to a satellite.

After being hoisted from the water in a specially designed cradle, the Great White Shark's eyes are covered and oxygen-rich water is passed over the gills while a wildlife vet takes blood samples. The SPOT tag is then directly mounted onto the dorsal fin.

Dr Ramon Bonfil, one of the leading scientists of the South African Great White Shark satellite-tagging project, shows the SPOT tags used. The computer screen shows the track of a Great White that ventured into Mozambican waters early on in the study.

The entire tagging procedure usually takes less than 10 minutes, after which the cradle is lowered and the shark is released back into the ocean, unharmed. The SPOT tag can clearly be seen on the dorsal fin as the shark swims away.

Nicole's journey

Nicole, by the time of her marathon swim an almost 4-m-long female Great White Shark, was first sighted and identified in September 1999 near Dyer Island. Her distinctive dorsal fin has triangular-shaped notches in the midsection of the trailing edge, both a large and a smaller tear indentation near the base, and a shredded, step-shaped upper portion near the tip. Ever since she was first identified, Nicole had followed a regular visitation pattern, returning to Dyer Island every year between July and December. Over the years, she had shown herself to be a confident shark with an inquisitive character. She would frequently swim up to the research boat, break the water surface with her head, and eye the boat's occupants. However, despite many seasons of seeing and studying her in the latter half of the year, her whereabouts during the first half of every year remained a mystery.

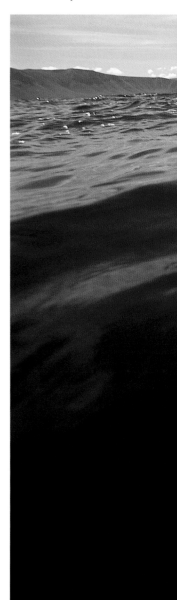

Nicole was tagged on the 7th of November 2003, near Dyer Island, with a PAT (see page 52), programmed to remain attached until the 28th of February 2004. In the early hours of that final day, a small, elongated canister floated to the surface off the western coast of Australia and began transmitting data gathered during several months spent largely underwater. This information was transmitted via satellite to the east coast of the USA where marine biologist Dr Ramon Bonfil, based at the Wildlife Conservation Society in New York, received the data and nearly choked on his breakfast bagel. He composed the following e-mail message to his colleagues: 'Nicole has gone to Australia!' Ninety-nine days after its deployment, her tag had popped up 11 000 km from where it was fitted – and the feisty Great White had made history.

Nicole's amazing journey across the ocean from Africa to Australia represented the first-ever recorded transoceanic migration for this shark species. Nicole also broke other records during her journey, diving regularly to great depths of 980 m, where the water temperature was a mere 3.4°C.

While Nicole was moving through coastal waters, she would spend two thirds of her time swimming in the top 5 m, whereas during her oceanic journey, she would swim up and down between the surface and the deep, spending 18 per cent of her time between 500 m and 750 m and 61 per cent between the surface and half a metre. Nicole travelled at a minimum speed of 4.7 km per hour during her migration to Australia, which is the fastest sustained long-distance speed known among sharks. This speed across the Indian Ocean also compares to that of some of the fastest-swimming tunas.

During her oceanic travels Nicole spent in excess of 60 per cent of her time swimming on or very close to the surface.

What urges Great White Sharks to travel such huge distances, and how do they manage to navigate across such a vast expanse of deep ocean? Could Nicole's repeated diving pattern be explained partly as a navigation tool? Was she getting her bearings from magnetic stimulae closer to the ocean floor (see page 22)? The strong preference for surface swimming during her oceanic migration represents a behavioural pattern previously unreported in Great White Sharks. And we can speculate that, like many vertebrates, Nicole could have been using visual stimuli, such as celestial cues, to navigate in a direct manner. It is also possible that Nicole used a combination of these 'signposts' – magnetic and celestial – to get her bearings and reach Australia.

CITES: what Nicole achieved

Considering the great regularity with which Nicole had been visiting Dyer Island for the five years prior to being tagged, we expected her to return from Australia sometime in July or August. However, with the spring of 2004 already drawing near, there was no sign of her from the vantage point of our research boat as we patrolled the waters around Dyer Island.

On 20 August 2004, despite an overcast sky, conditions were ideal: a light breeze drifting over a flat ocean. After hours of waiting, a dark shadow appeared in the water, 20 m from the boat. As the dorsal fin of a Great White Shark emerged, we were overjoyed to identify it as Nicole's. In just over nine months, Nicole had swum from South Africa to Australia (and perhaps further) and back – a journey of over 22 000 km.

Despite our continued fieldwork efforts and the regularity of her annual visits to South Africa from 1999 to 2004, we failed to observe Nicole during 2005. We do not know for certain why she did not return to South Africa in 2005, but we do have theories. At almost

Even the roughest of seas are no match for a Great White and these sharks can maintain speeds of at least 4.7 km per hour over long distances. In short bursts, they can even clock 50 km per hour.

4 m in length, Nicole was close to reaching maturity, and perhaps migratory and habitat preferences are age related. There could also be more sinister reasons, such as Nicole's having perished on a long line or in a gill net. It is also possible that she did make an appearance but was missed by us and other scientists.

Unfortunately, we will never know what transpired, and why she did not maintain her pattern of migrating back to South Africa, but we await her return with anticipation.

The 13th meeting of the Conference of Parties of CITES was held at the beginning of October 2004 in Bangkok, Thailand. On 12 October 2004, the 166 members voted on the joint proposal to list the Great White Shark on CITES Appendix II. This long-awaited proposal was accepted, by secret ballot, with a 72 per cent majority (87 in favour, 34 opposed and 9 abstentions). This milestone for Great White Shark conservation was achieved, to a large extent, by the proof that the species does indeed leave the protected waters of the few countries that have conservation legislation in place on a national level.

GREAT WHITES IN DEEP TROUBLE

Conservation status

Great White Sharks grow slowly, mature late and have a low reproduction rate, all elements of what is termed a 'K-selected species' – one that is easily threatened by unnatural mortalities. Evidence of their threatened status is the decline in the bycatch of Great Whites in the northwest Atlantic pelagic longline fishery by between 60 and 90 per cent over the past four decades. Today, Great White Sharks are not only listed on CITES, but also on the IUCN (International Union for the Conservation of Nature and Natural Resources) Red List of Threatened Species as *Vulnerable*. Great White Sharks are at the top of the marine food chain, and occupy an important and strategic role in the marine ecosystem. Without Great White Sharks, the balance of life would tip and the health of our oceans deteriorate.

Threats to Great White Sharks

Despite the groundbreaking 2005 CITES victory, Great White Sharks still face many threats, both in local as well as in foreign and international waters.

HOOKS OF DEATH

The Indian Ocean teems with long-line fleets that deploy hundreds of kilometres of line, set with thousands of baited hooks. While these target tuna and swordfish, hundreds of millions of sharks are also caught. Shark meat does not fetch high prices, but the fins, for use in shark-fin soup, have an extremely high value, fetching hundreds of dollars per kilogram in Asian markets. Since freezer space on fishing boats is limited, fishermen readily cut off the fins before throwing the live, maimed shark overboard. The number of Great White Sharks killed in this way is not known, but a recent genetic study has shown that out of one ton of confiscated fins, 21 sets belonged to Great Whites.

ILLEGAL TRADE AND POACHING

A quick search on the Internet reveals an extensive market for Great White products, where teeth sell for $30–$500 on some on-line shopping sites (some of these sellers have distinctly South African e-mail addresses). The exact source of illegal Great White products cannot be identified clearly, but it is likely that some small-scale poaching of Great White Sharks still occurs off the South African coast. This trade is reputedly perpetrated by abalone-poaching syndicates, but it is also known that jaws and teeth taken from sharks killed before 1991 are being sold.

SHARK NETS

One 'fishery' continues, legally, to catch and kill Great Whites along the KwaZulu-Natal coast: the Natal Sharks Board is responsible for maintaining over 40 km of gill nets along the shore to protect swimmers and surfers from sharks. Contrary to popular belief, the nets don't create an impenetrable barrier, but catch as many sharks as possible, reducing the shark population and hence the incidence of shark bites. Each year, between 20 and 60 Great White Sharks are caught and, prior to 1993, any Great White found alive in the nets was destroyed. Today, those that survive are quickly released.

AQUACULTURE

Fish farming carried out in offshore pens needs to be properly regulated, otherwise it can easily become a threat to marine life. In 2004 a Norwegian salmon farm was established near Dyer Island, an area that is home to the highest known concentrations of Great Whites in the world. This farm is still in a pilot phase, but, if successful, could result in hundreds of netted pens – each a potential death trap – in operation near Great White hot spots. In Australia, in five years, nine Great Whites were caught in similar pens used by tuna farms. Six of these sharks were killed and three were found already dead – a 100 per cent mortality rate. Fish farming near Great White hot spots is akin to ranching sheep in Kruger National Park. It sets up conflict between farmers and predators, in which the predator will always lose.

How you can help to protect Great Whites

1 If you want to buy shark teeth, it is imperative that they are fossilised teeth, of which there is an almost unlimited supply available for sale (or for collection on certain beaches), legally, without harming shark populations.
2 Report any Great White products you encounter offered for sale in South Africa to the White Shark Trust (**www.whitesharktrust.org**), which will then pass on this information to the appropriate authorities.
3 Write letters to government expressing your concern about South Africa's shark populations, and demand that all shark fishing, as well as the landing of any shark products by foreign vessels in South African ports, is made illegal. The income earned by catching and killing sharks is just a fraction of what they are worth in the ecotourism and diving arena.
4 Go cage diving and support an industry that has made the Great White Shark worth more alive than dead (see page 60).

6 SHARK WATCHING

Steven Spielberg's 1975 film, *JAWS*, terrified audiences while breaking all box-office records of the day. The highly successful and widely acclaimed film grossed in excess of 260 million dollars, but *JAWS* was to be a catastrophe for the Great White Shark. The film's impact was unprecedented as 'shark-attack' hysteria gripped the film-going world. The Great White Shark went from being considered – at most – an obscure ocean dweller to a man-eating monster with a lust for wanton killing. In the wake of the film followed a Great White killing frenzy motivated by fear, with anglers and trophy hunters in the USA, Australia and South Africa setting out to sea to bring back as many large Great Whites as possible. As the death toll mounted, marine biologists grew concerned about the impact that this extended fishing effort was having and, with every passing year, the evidence increasingly showed

Worth more alive than dead

In 1991, the tide of destruction of Great Whites was stemmed when South Africa became the first nation in the world to proclaim them a protected species. Namibia, Malta, Australia and the USA followed suit in the succeeding decade, putting an almost immediate end to most of the trophy fishing and retaliatory killings of Great White Sharks. Just a few years before this, Australian diver Rodney Fox took another visionary step towards shark conservation: he launched the first venture in the world taking tourists out to sea to view and cage dive with Great White Sharks off the coast of South Australia.

The first such operations were launched in South Africa soon after the species became protected, with many one-time Great White hunters trading in their fishing rods for diving cages and becoming the driving force of this new-found industry. Many doubted whether these ventures that sprang up around Dyer and Seal Islands would ultimately prove to be successful, but the *JAWS*-related notoriety, originally to the sharks' detriment, now ensured that people would travel half way across the world to observe the Great White Shark in the wild. Great White diving was a hit and grew from humble beginnings to a multimillion-dollar industry in a matter of a few years, for the first time making the Great White worth exponentially more alive than dead.

In this chapter we take a look at the current practices of Great White Shark tourism in South Africa, review relevant conservation legislation and discuss some controversial practices.

Today, tens of thousands of tourists travel from all corners of the globe to South Africa to view Great White Sharks from the safety of a cage.

Cage diving – taking the plunge

At present, one can go Great White watching at three South African locations: Dyer Island, Seal Island in False Bay and Seal Island off Mossel Bay. Unlike the Neptune Islands off South Australia and Guadalupe Island off Mexico, which lie far offshore, the South African Great White hot spots are unique in that they can be reached by day boats in under an hour. All three sites are in close proximity to Cape fur seal colonies, which is why they attract such high concentrations of Great White Sharks (see chapters 3 and 4, pages 26–49).

Once at the spot, the boat anchors and begins to chum the water with a pungent brew of fish oils, finely minced sardines, tuna and puréed shark livers, creating a slick that spreads from the boat with the prevailing currents and winds. Great Whites patrolling in the area pick up the scent and use their sophisticated sense of smell to follow the chum slick upstream to its source. Sharks sometimes arrive within minutes, while at other times, hours can pass without so much as a dorsal fin in sight. When they do arrive, they are often very cautious, and only once they appear relaxed around the boat is a cage lowered into the water. At the same time, the divers put on their wetsuits (an essential piece of

The prospect of capturing Great Whites on film lures photographers – both amateur and professional – from all over the world to South Africa, making it the world's premier shark-tourism destination.

Killing sharks to watch sharks?

Many tourism operators use the livers of other sharks to attract Great Whites to their boats. These livers are usually taken from soup-fin and sevengill (or broadnose) sharks fished on a commercial basis primarily for their meat and fins. Until very recently, shark livers had no commercial value and were given away freely; today, however, due to the great demand for them by the Great White tourism industry, there is a high commercial value attached to them, contributing substantially to the worth of these sharks. However, there is no such thing as a sustainable shark fishery as *all* sharks are vulnerable to overexploitation and extinction.

By adding commercial value to sharks through harvesting their livers, the fishing of these animals is perpetuated when it should, in fact, be stopped. Furthermore, there are rumours circulating that some fishermen are now specifically targeting sevengill sharks just for their livers. From an ecotourism perspective, it seems hypocritical that we should be encouraging the killing of one shark species so that tourists can view, learn about, appreciate and help to conserve another. The viability of other sources of attractants from more sustainable marine stocks must urgently be investigated.

equipment provided by the operators since the water temperature is often below 15°C) and quietly enter the cage so as not to scare the sharks away. The Great Whites are then lured closer to the cage by a piece of bait, often shark meat or a tuna head attached to a rope. In the past, the wire mesh cages were circular and could accommodate only a single diver. Today, the industry standard is a much larger rectangular cage that holds between four and six divers.

The cage is attached to one side of the boat and never leaves the surface. The divers, equipped with masks and weight belts, wait, heads above water, until the dive master tells them that a shark is approaching, and from which direction. He signals to them to take a deep breath and submerge. Some operations allow qualified divers to use scuba regulators, and, in clear water, this can be a great advantage for those who are suitably qualified. However, when the visibility is not very good, being submerged in this way can put one at a disadvantage as, without the dive master's directions, it is easy to miss the approach of fast-swimming sharks. On most days throughout the year, perhaps with the exception of the months of February and March, one can expect to see at least one shark; and during the southern hemisphere's winter months, there have been extraordinary outings during which more than 25 Great White Sharks have been spotted in just a few hours.

Is cage diving safe?

A question frequently asked by people interested in going Great White watching is whether it is dangerous. While in the early days of Great White tourism, cages and boats of questionable quality were used, standards today are exceptionally high, with stringent safety protocols, tried and tested equipment, well-trained guides and experienced skippers. The diving cages have become more sturdy over the years, but this is not because sharks were biting them – Great Whites are actually wary of a cage filled with noisy divers. The cages have been improved and strengthened, as well as enlarged so as to accommodate a greater number of people to view the sharks at a time.

For those who do not want to venture into the cage, viewing sharks from specially designed platforms on boats is also a richly rewarding experience. Great Whites tend to be very active on the surface around the boats and, while some tourists struggle to get into wet suits and into the cage to catch a glimpse of a shark, those who have chosen to remain above water get a much longer and more complete view of all the action. Consequently, even those diving should ensure that they leave some time for surface viewing – before or after a session in the cage.

Great sharks, greater controversy

Over the years, since Great White Shark tourism kicked off in South Africa, the cage-diving industry in the region has not been without controversy, or controversial figures, for that matter. To date, the biggest single bone of contention has been the claim that cage diving encourages Great Whites to bite people (see page 68). There are, however, several other issues that Great White Shark tourists should be aware of, including 'free diving' (encountering Great Whites outside a cage) and 'mouth opening'.

'Free diving'

Permit conditions for shark tourism clearly state that all diving has to be carried out within the confines of a cage and that Great Whites may not be attracted by chum or food for the purpose of free diving with them.

However, before this law came into effect, a few select and very experienced people pioneered the art of diving with Great Whites outside the safety of a cage. Their initial motivation was curiosity and a pioneering spirit. It put to the test what many insiders have known for a long time, a contention that appears to have been ignored by the rest of the world: that Great Whites are not wanton killers eager to bite anything in their path and that, in the right circumstances, it is possible for a person to swim freely with a Great White. At first, it was a very personal journey for these divers, and only when television producers and photographers got wind of the fact that there were people at the southern tip of Africa free swimming with Great Whites did the rest of the world begin to take note.

A host of films and magazine articles featuring free diving started to appear, which did much to improve the image of the Great White Shark. It's clear that, initially, free diving helped educate the general public about Great Whites, and significantly enhanced efforts to conserve the species.

This initial boon, however, was short-lived. As news of successful free-diving operations spread, some operators even started to offer tourists the opportunity to dive outside of the cage. Those who have spent a great deal of time with sharks, such as experienced professional film-makers and photographers, are perhaps justified in being allowed to free dive in the company of experts; inviting a tourist to do so, regardless of diving experience, is taking a senseless risk, however. A single bad incident could set back all the positive gains of free diving and reinstate the Great White's negative image.

We believe that there is a time and place for free diving today – but definitely not in the tourism arena. Those with the necessary experience to free dive can contribute valuable data in the realm of behavioural research, preferably working in tandem with trained marine biologists in order to establish and adhere to proper scientific protocols.

'Mouth opening'

From the late 1990s onwards, some cage-diving operators started to touch Great White Sharks on their snout to trigger a strange reaction. When touched like this, the shark will rear out of the water and open its mouth wide, displaying its dagger-like teeth to the fullest extent. It is said that this behaviour was discovered when a Great White Shark was trying to bite one of the boat's engines and the crew tried to push it away by its snout.

Conservation legislation

The Great White Shark cage-diving code of conduct (as set out by South Africa's Marine and Coastal Management) prohibits the feeding of Great Whites. It happens that even the most careful operator will lose the occasional piece of bait to a swift shark. However, if sharks get hold of and eat the bait more than a few times during an outing, it suggests that the operator is feeding them in order to give the tourists a more dramatic, 'JAWS-type' show. It is not necessary to watch a Great White thrashing around at the end of a bait rope in order to appreciate the spectacle. After all, cage diving is not an 'extreme sport', but a wildlife-watching experience.

Even if sharks are treated with care, they can still injure themselves on the boats' propellers, for they are drawn to them by the metal's electromagnetic discharges. Responsible operators prevent such injuries by covering the engines and propellers with recycled conveyer-belt material.

When considering cage diving, first check whether the operator feeds the sharks and covers his boat's engines. If you witness unethical practices, report them to the guide or captain, or to the Nature Conservation authorities or Marine and Coastal Management.

Why the shark reacts in this manner when touched is still a mystery, but it could be an over-stimulation of its sensory system, which largely lies embedded in the snout. This behaviour could also be a protective reflex for sharks in that the snout is their blind spot; by arching their head backwards and opening their mouth wide, they threaten to bite whatever may be touching their snout.

Soon film crews and photographers got wind of this behaviour and images of sharks displaying their gaping jaws above the water were everywhere, including on the cover of the April 2000 issue of *National Geographic*. As tourist interest grew, this behaviour modification was integrated into daily Great White tourist trips, with many guides trying to open as many mouths as possible for the tourist cameras. Those in the know carry out this act gently and sensitively, and some sharks actually appear to enjoy being touched as they keep returning to the same position at the back of the boat for hours. Unfortunately, however, some operators forcefully grab sharks by the nose and wrestle with them instead of simply touching them. Not only does touching sharks' noses (or any other part of the animal) set a bad example for tourists but, more importantly, this trick creates a perception about Great Whites that is not in line with the true nature of the species. Such apparently aggressive images help create the impression that the Great White Shark is on the offensive, punching through the water with jaws agape. In fact, after reacting so dramatically, the shark simply falls backwards into the water. In 2002 the practice of touching sharks was banned.

Great White Sharks are not as dangerous as we often are led to believe. Over the last 83 years, there have been only 22 fatalities attributed to Great White bites in South African waters.

Great White bites in South Africa (1922–2005)

Our analysis of Great White bites encompasses the period between 1922 and 2005. However, it should be noted that record keeping and reporting occurred at much lower levels in the earlier years of this period, so data that predates 1960, in particular, could underestimate the actual figures.

The earliest record of a Great White bite in South African waters was in 1922 and occurred in False Bay, where a swimmer sustained minor injuries to his abdominal region. Between that first recorded bite and 31 December 2005, a period of 83 years, Great Whites were implicated in a further 89 incidents, of which 22 were fatal. To put this figure in perspective, in 2004 alone there were 560 incidents of drowning in South Africa, while in 2000, 32 485 people were murdered and 18 446 died in road traffic accidents.

In South Africa, Great White bites have been reported from all coastal provinces except the Northern Cape. Between 1922 and 2005, 33 per cent of all bites occurred in the Eastern Cape, 49 per cent in the Western Cape and 18 per cent in KwaZulu-Natal. Surfers (including bodyboarders) were the most frequent Great White bite victims, making up 41 per cent. Swimmers and spear fishermen accounted for 23 per cent each, free divers/snorkellers for 6 per cent, surf skiers for 4 per cent, and scuba divers for 3 per cent. From the earliest recorded Great White bite to the present day there has been a noticeable increase in incidents. For example, while between 1921 and 1950 there were, on average, three bites

The distinctive jaw and teeth imprint of a large Great White Shark on the tail end of a board belonging to an East London surfer.

In recent years surfing has been transformed from an extreme sport into a mainstream activity, exponentially increasing the number of participants. Today, surfers and bodyboarders make up the highest number of Great White Shark bite victims, 41 per cent of the total.

attributed to Great White Sharks per decade, between 1951 and 1970 this doubled to six and continued to increase in the following years. Between 1981 and 1990 there were 25 Great White Shark bites, an all-time high, decreasing only slightly between 1991 and 2000 when 23 incidents were reported. For the first half of this decade there have been 11 reported Great White bites.

The population of South Africa has increased from 13.5 million in 1950 to more than 46 million in 2005. Between 1980 and 2000 it is estimated that the number of people to use the False Bay shoreline increased from 1.7 to 3.6 million. A more detailed comparison of beach attendance reveals that in 1967 an average of about 5 000 people used False Bay's beaches, while in 1987 this figure increased by over 350 per cent to nearly 23 000. While more up-to-date data is not available, in terms of world trends, beach attendance along the California coast, for example, doubled between 1994 and 2005. Research suggests that beach attendance has increased similarly along the South African coastline. One must also take into account that, since the end of apartheid in 1994, a time when most beaches were reserved for a small number of white people only, a far greater number of people now has access to all beaches.

Many South African beachgoers are actively engaged in water-sport activities, and water sports have grown in popularity in recent years. Surfing, in particular, has transformed from an extreme sport practised by a few hardened adherents to a mainstream sporting activity, involving tens of thousands of participants. Scuba diving, too, has mirrored this trend, and between 1990 and 2005 the number of scuba divers certified by the Professional Association of Diving Instructors (PADI) increased from four million to more than 10 million people worldwide. In South Africa, the number of divers has also increased dramatically.

An exponential growth in the number of people using the sea will obviously increase the likelihood of encounters between humans and Great Whites and, correspondingly, bites resulting from such encounters. Furthermore, with the manufacture of better wetsuits, the time spent in the water by surfers or spear fishermen has also increased significantly.

Only three per cent of all Great White bite victims are scuba divers. The advantage they have over surfers is that they can see the shark long before it decides to investigate them more closely.

Why do Great Whites bite people?

We cannot say with utmost certainty why Great White Sharks bite people. Our poor knowledge of the behaviour of this apex predator means we have little understanding as to what their primary motivation might be. Despite such uncertainty, experts have put forward several theories as to why people are sometimes bitten by Great White Sharks, and they help shed light on at least some of the incidents.

Investigatory/curiosity theory

In Great White research circles, it is commonly believed that most of the time Great Whites do not approach humans for hunting purposes, but rather out of curiosity. They have often been observed calmly circling unfamiliar objects before moving in to investigate more closely. Unable to identify the novel object they have encountered with their other senses, they must now rely on their remaining tactile sense, taste.

A Great White's taste organs are situated in the roof of the mouth and, by giving an unidentified object a light nip, a shark can gain further information about it. Injuries after such bites are usually minor, as the tasting procedure requires minimal force. Investigatory bites also appear to happen on a regular basis to seabirds such as penguins (see chapter 3, page 35), as well as to inanimate objects like kayaks, boats and paddle skis.

Mistaken identity theory

Great Whites can sense the presence of a person in the ocean long before the person is able to detect the shark (see page 20). They can detect sounds – like those made by people swimming or splashing in the water – over distances of hundreds of metres, even kilometres. A shark can smell even just a few drops of blood and other bodily fluids from at least 100 m away. At a distance of up to 100 m, a Great White can sense a person by means of pressure-sensitive receptors in its lateral line, which can detect ripples and even the smallest vibration in the water (see page 22). A Great White Shark's vision, too, is excellent, and in clear water it can probably see a person from far beyond the limits of our own vision. However, being able to *detect* a person from a great distance and correctly *identify* it are two different things.

Great whites are unlikely to mistake a person for a Cape fur seal in clear water, but when the sea is murky, it is possible that they may, occasionally, mistake a human for their usual prey.

Great White Sharks have roamed the oceans for millions of years and evolved their sophisticated array of senses in parallel with their preferred prey of seals, dolphins and tuna, all of which have been around for at least 20 million years. Humans are relative newcomers to the planet and, while fossils of the earliest *Homo sapiens* date back 500 000 years, it is only in the last 50 years or so that we have developed the technology to enable us to spend extended periods of time in cold water. Most Great White Sharks will therefore be unfamiliar with what a human is, and it is likely that divers, surfers and bathers send out a very different sense signature from those of fish or seals.

It is, however, possible, when visibility is marginal, when waves and surf cause background noise, and when other prey is in the vicinity, that there is enough similarity between a human's sense signatures and those of the Great White's normal prey to trigger its hunting instinct. The shark will then rush at the person, usually from below to disguise its approach, and deliver a first bite. Its mouth is lined with an array of microscopic taste buds, which, it is believed, can distinguish basic combinations of flavours. Some researchers believe that the taste buds are even able to detect the calorific value of any potential prey, informing the shark of the ratio of nutritious fat (suggesting, perhaps, a seal) versus non-nutritious bone and muscle (such as that of a person). When a Great White's taste buds come into contact with a person or a surfboard, they should send an immediate, clear signal to the shark that it has made a mistake and is not hunting its preferred prey. This may account for the many cases in which people have sustained minor tissue damage only – rather than suffered the full-strength bite of the Great White, so powerful that it can snap a person in half – before being released.

Feeding theory

Among Great White Shark-bite victims, the feeding bite is least common. On the rare occasions that, instead of tentatively tasting and then releasing the person, a shark delivers a full bite and subsequently begins feeding, it is clear that the shark considers humans to be suitable prey. There is only one confirmed account of this behaviour in South Africa. In April 1971, at Buffels Bay near Knysna, a swimmer was struck hard by a Great White Shark that returned and repeatedly took bites out of the already dead victim.

There are a further few incidents where it is strongly suspected that Great Whites did feed on or consume a person. However, because of a lack of direct evidence, other factors such as strong currents and/or a high number of scavengers in the area cannot be ruled out as accounting for the disappearance of a victim's body.

Why do some Great Whites decide to feed on humans when the majority of this species seemingly does not? We do not know, but can draw parallels with the circumstances often suspected of prompting some terrestrial predators, such as tigers and lions, to become man-eaters (see page 77).

The immediate question is whether the few Great White Sharks that actually eat their victims are old or injured, or are healthy individuals in their prime that develop a taste for human flesh and are the perpetrators of repeat incidents. Again, because of the rarity of such incidents and because the shark responsible is only very rarely caught and positively identified as the perpetrator, the characteristics of Great White Sharks that bite and eat people are not known. However, it is highly unlikely that a Great White could successfully survive mainly on human prey for long; not only is the shark much larger than, say, a tiger, lion or leopard, requiring a much higher energy intake, but it is also not endowed with dexterous paws to eat selectively by consuming only the nutritious pieces. By design, a Great White would have to consume a person whole, utilising valuable energy to digest bones and muscles that, compared to fat, have a low nutritional value, and from which the shark would gain very little energy.

If Great Whites really did develop a taste for humans, the carnage and loss of life would be of epidemic proportions.

LEGENDARY MAN-EATERS

Unlike Great White Sharks, which are best described as 'occasional man biters', terrestrial carnivores in some parts of the world deserve the 'man-eater' label. Although predation of humans by big cats is very rare, tigers and lions are the worst offenders. In the Sundarbans, a tidal region draped in mangrove forests and located in the far south of Bangladesh, tigers killed at least 400 people between 1956 and 1970. In neighbouring India, just 10 tigers were responsible for eating no fewer than 650 people in less than five years. In Africa lions, too, have been known to kill and eat people and in the early 20th century, two male lions ate more than 30 railroad workers in Tsavo, Kenya. Near the Tanzanian town of Njombe a pride of lions killed more than 1 000 people over a 15-year period in the 1930s. In 1997 lions in and around the Kruger National Park killed 11 immigrants that were illegally crossing into South Africa from Mozambique. Even chimpanzees occasionally hunt people, and at least eight children were killed and partially eaten in Uganda and Tanzania over a seven-year period.

Man-eating is much more widespread on land than in the ocean. It could be that, because humans have been an integral part of the terrestrial food chain for so much longer than the marine equivalent, terrestrial predators in some regions recognise us as bona fide prey. But there may also be more immediate reasons for a tiger or a lion to hunt and eat humans: some animals implicated in such incidents have been very old or injured and unable to catch their normal prey, and so have turned to hunting people in their struggle to survive.

However more often than not, individuals that have eaten humans have been in prime condition. Perhaps they inadvertently discovered how vulnerable people really are and took to this practice because it was profitable, perhaps subsequently even passing on this feeding 'culture' to future generations.

Social/defensive theory

Great Whites do not communicate through sound but use a social repertoire of body posturing and biting. However, research on the social behaviour of the species is in its infancy and the theories outlined below are based largely on anecdotal evidence.

Great Whites are not territorial and do not defend a fixed piece of ocean 'real estate' from competitors. They do, however, defend their 'personal space' as well as prey items. For example, when two Great Whites meet one another, the smaller and/or less dominant one will usually give way to the larger, or dominant individual. If neither backs off or swims away, displays of parallel and circular swimming and jaw gaping have been known to follow. If this fails then one of the sharks, presumably the more dominant one, will attack and bite or rake its teeth across the other shark's body. Most of the time injuries resulting from social bites are minor, but there have been a few instances in which a Great White has seriously injured or killed another. It is, therefore, plausible that a human who intrudes into the Great White's realm, and who fails to respond by withdrawing from the area, might trigger the shark to bite in defence of its space. Although most humans would be unlikely to interpret shark body language correctly, in the majority of cases the victim would not even be aware of the shark's presence until bitten. When in the vicinity of a food source such as seals or fish, a Great White might conceivably view a person as a competitor and attempt to chase them away from the area.

LEFT: Two Great Whites encounter one another around the bait put out by a cage-diving boat. However, instead of plunging into a feeding frenzy, the smaller shark gives way to the larger, more dominant individual. *ABOVE:* Great Whites are not territorial but do defend their personal space and maintain a minimum distance from nearby conspecifics.

GREAT WHITE BITES

8 CAGE DIVING: THE IMPACT

Having someone killed by a Great White Shark in close proximity to where one surfs, swims or dives can be a traumatic experience and, despite shark bites occurring so infrequently, can unearth more extreme emotions than those aroused in the wake of a road accident or natural disaster.

The fear of being injured by a predator in the ocean is disproportionately strong, and studies have shown that simply hearing the word 'shark' causes a measurable increase in people's heart rate and muscle tension. While the general public may tolerate infrequent shark-bite incidents spread out over many years and generally accept them as 'freak accidents', they react strongly, emotionally and often irrationally once such occurrences are perceived to be more regular.

To date, science lacks an answer as to why shark bites are so much higher in some years than in others, but it is likely that an array of oceanographic and ecological factors are responsible for suddenly bringing more (or fewer) sharks into contact with people. However, often the public needs a more tangible explanation, and in 1998 the fledgling Great White Shark tourism industry was blamed for the increase in bites by attracting more Great Whites close to shore and by conditioning sharks to associate people with food. The number of shark bites returned to normal levels in the years that followed, and Great White Shark tourism continued, largely unhindered.

The season of July and August 2001 became known as the 'Summer of the Shark', after *Time* magazine ran this as a sensational headline on its front cover. The media took up the cry and portrayed the notion that the number of shark bites, particularly off the east coast of the USA, was significantly higher than normal. However, in 2001 worldwide shark-incident statistics were actually below average. Nonetheless, the largely media-fuelled shark-bite frenzy continued unabated, particularly in the state of Florida, USA, which has always been the world's number one shark-bite hot spot.

Just as in South Africa in 1998, when people were desperately looking for explanations as to why sharks bite people, Americans blamed a small tourism industry that takes scuba divers on organised shark dives off Florida. Despite many experts disagreeing with the notion that shark-feeding activities were responsible for any of these shark incidents, shark diving was banned a year later, largely to satisfy public opinion.

In December 2002, South Africa too began to feel the repercussions of the 'Summer of the Shark' after a free diver was seriously bitten off the western shores of the Cape Peninsula. The call to ban Great White cage diving to guard against shark bites was heard again. A year later, a Great White fatally injured a young bodyboarder at Noordhoek. In April of the following year, a bodyboarder lost a leg to a Great White at Muizenberg. Then, in June, a Great White near Dyer Island killed a suspected abalone poacher and, in November, a swimmer was taken just off Fish Hoek. With every incident, the number of media reports and the level of public concern grew dramatically. In 2005 there were two confirmed incidents, one a fatal bite on a spear fisherman.

Seven Great White bites – four of them fatal – in three years, along just 200 km of coast, traumatised the local population. Fuelled by sensationalism, the public called for a ban on all Great White Shark tourism activities. Many called for the installation of shark gill nets along the affected coast, and also advocated shark-hunting expeditions, or trophy fishing, which would fill tourism coffers.

Arguments for and against cage diving

Arguments for and against cage diving have raged ever since its inception in 1991. A nervous and sometimes uninformed sector of the public has campaigned vociferously to bring an end to the activity, while committed divers and cage-diving operators, often with vested interests in continuing their livelihood, have sought to defend the practice.

Chumming: does it attract more sharks?

We might draw the conclusion that if cage-diving boats ladle bucket-loads of chum into the ocean on a daily basis they must, in some way, be responsible for Great Whites biting and even killing people. Surely this practice attracts more Great Whites closer to shore? However, all three Great White viewing locations in South Africa have been chosen precisely because they are already home to naturally high concentrations of these sharks, which congregate there to be in the immediate vicinity of large seal colonies. Kilometre-long slicks of seal faeces and other bodily secretions stream outwards from these islands, easily overpowering in strength and area the chumming by boats. In short, the tourism boats are focused on attracting only those sharks that are already in the area and are unlikely to attract additional sharks from further afield.

Seal colonies create kilometre-long natural 'chum slicks' that easily overpower the chumming churned out by tourism operators.

Great White bites – before and after cage diving

- In the 14 years prior to the beginning of cage diving (1978), 30 Great White Shark bites were recorded in South Africa, while in the subsequent 14 years during which shark tourism has been taking place, there were 32 bites.
- The ratio of bites between the western and eastern Cape coasts has remained the same, despite Great White Shark tourism being practised only in the former. In False Bay and along the west coast of the Cape Peninsula, the area perceived to have been impacted the most, there has been only a 25% increase in the number of bites, a figure in line with the increase in ocean users.
- If Great Whites were making an association between cage divers and food, one would expect an increase in bites on people engaged in similar underwater activities. However, bites on divers have decreased by almost 50 per cent, while those involving surfers have increased by 30 per cent.

Conditioned to bite?

Some people believe that shark tourism conditions Great White Sharks to associate people with food and, in turn, to become aggressive in the presence of people and boats.

'Pavlov's shark'

It is worth referring to the experiments that the famous Russian scientist Ivan Pavlov conducted on his dog. For weeks, without fail, each time Pavlov fed his dog he also rang a bell. Soon the dog was able to associate the ringing of the bell with the delivery of food, and would begin to salivate when just the bell was rung. In 1903 Pavlov published his results, calling this learning process 'conditioning', in which the dog's nervous system comes to associate the sound of a bell with food.

Could sharks become conditioned in the same way? Dr Eugenie Clark of Florida's Mote Marine Laboratory (formerly Cape Haze Marine Laboratory) performed the first conditioning experiments in 1959 on two adult lemon sharks. She lowered a white plywood target into a large shark enclosure at their regular feeding time. Several pieces of fish were attached to the plywood in such a manner that the sharks had to touch the target with their snout when taking food. Every time they took food, a submerged bell would ring. After six weeks of repeating this exercise on a daily basis, the target was lowered again, but this time without the food attached. The sharks nonetheless swam up to and touched the target hard enough to set off the bell, for which they were rewarded by being given pieces of fish. The fish, however, was attached to a string and the sharks were given only 10 seconds to eat the fish before it was taken away. After only one week, both lemon sharks were successfully conditioned to press the target and then take the food offered within 10 seconds.

At this stage, a seasonal drop in water temperature resulted in the sharks losing interest in food, and experiments proceeded again only after 10 weeks. In spite of the break in routine, the sharks readily resumed pressing the target and taking the food.

While this demonstrates that conditioning of sharks is possible, it must be remembered that this research was carried out on captive animals under controlled conditions. In reality, things seldom run so smoothly. In his dog-conditioning experiments, Pavlov found that the conditioned reflex will be repressed if the stimulus proves 'wrong' too often: if the bell sounds repeatedly and no food appears, the dog eventually stops salivating at the sound. In the same way, conditioning of sharks is only possible if they are frequently fed bait; and it is theoretically not possible for sharks to become conditioned to anticipate a meal through chumming alone, since the sharks attracted in this way do not regularly receive food rewards. The code of conduct to which all Great White Shark tourism operators subscribe (see chapter 6) clearly prohibits the feeding of sharks: the teaser bait at the end of a long rope is supposed to be used only to keep the sharks' interest and guide them closer to the cage. While even the most careful and ethical operator will occasionally lose a piece of bait to a swift shark, at no time are sharks supposed to catch and actually consume the bait, and thus be rewarded.

Some operators, however, do intentionally feed Great Whites, because most sharks are actually very wary of boats, and feeding keeps them around for longer. What about these operators who flaunt the legislation – are they causing some sharks to become conditioned to asociate food with humans?

Pleasure versus pain

Dr Eugenie Clark of Mote Marine Laboratory also studied the effects of negative associations in her experiments with lemon sharks. Clark found that when a shark had a bad experience, for example when she startled it by employing a different-coloured target, it would refuse to touch the target. It seemed as though all conditioning was lost when the strictly controlled environment changed even slightly.

In further conditioning experiments, again using lemon sharks, Dr Samuel 'Doc' Gruber from the University of Miami and the Bimini Biological Field Station, experimented using pain – not rewards – as a trigger. He noticed that every time he gave a shark a light electric shock, it winked. He then flashed a light before every jolt. After 100 such pairings of the light and the electric shock, the light alone was enough to make the shark wink (it takes a cat around 800 such trials to make the same connections).

When a Great White approaches a boat and cage and gets a piece of bait, it may feel rewarded for its behaviour. However, if at the next approach the stimuli are different or the association with coming to the boat is negative, the shark may be persuaded

Ethical Great White tourism operators rely on the teaser bait only to guide the shark close to the cage to ensure a good sighting, but unscrupulous companies feed large quantities of bait to keep wary and nervous sharks around their boats for longer.

not to associate boats with a ready source of food. It might take no more than the shark's bumping into the cage or reacting to the sudden movement of a person on the boat to break such an association.

Notably, most of the sharks around Dyer Island, the busiest cage-diving location off our coasts, are not residential and usually stay at the island for no more than a few weeks before moving on. Sharks stay at the other two locations – Seal Island in False Bay and Seal Island in Mossel Bay – for longer periods; but the same shark would have to be fed again and again, without any negative interference, for it to establish a firm association between cage-diving activities and a readily available source of food. To

date, only short-term behavioural changes, such as some sharks arriving at boats more quickly, have been observed in the industry.

In a worst-case scenario, where some Great Whites might indeed have become conditioned to associate boats with food, sharks would repeatedly be exposed to the sounds and sensations of boat motors, anchors dropping and, of course, chumming. However, researchers are unclear as to how this would lead to Great Whites biting more people more frequently. In the same way that lions or elephants do not necessarily associate humans with motor vehicles, and probably only notice them when they get out of their cars, it is unlikely that sharks associate people inside a metal cage with scuba divers or surfers in the ocean.

Despite claims that towing seal-shaped decoys to elicit spectacular breaches conditions sharks to bite surfers and bodyboarders, all evidence points to the contrary. As with chumming, there is no food or other reward and, in fact, the practice should discourage sharks from biting anything that does not exactly resemble their normal prey.

Another practice of some Great White operators that has been criticised is towing a seal-shaped decoy through the water to elicit spectacular breaches. Critics claim that this might encourage Great White Sharks to attack surfers and bodyboarders, whose silhouetted shape the towed decoy is said to resemble. A Great White Shark spotting such a decoy would launch a hunt on what it considers to be a seal swimming on the surface – only to find that it is, in fact, a smelly old piece of carpet or foam. The attack would have used up precious energy and yielded no food. If anything, towing decoys should discourage sharks from biting anything that does not look entirely like the food they normally eat.

Tourism without chumming?

Despite evidence not supporting claims that there is a link between Great White Shark tourism and Great Whites biting people with increased frequency, some still believe that there are other reasons why Great White tourism, in its present form, is nonetheless undesirable.

In comparison to terrestrial game viewing, the manner in which Great White Shark watching is carried out is indeed archaic. Over the years, baiting and feeding of terrestrial animals has stopped in most places. It has been advocated that chumming and baiting of Great White Sharks should likewise be abandoned, and that viewing be conducted along similar principles to whale watching. In principal, this is the ideal ecotourism scenario.

However, where chum-less Great White safaris have been attempted, such as in the Farallon Islands off the California Coast, they have enjoyed only limited success because of low sighting frequencies. There is one location where this type of Great White tourism would be feasible in South Africa: Seal Island in False Bay where, during the winter months, viewing natural Great White Shark predations on Cape fur seals is successfully being offered by two operators.

So why can't all Great White Shark tours be run in this manner? Seal Island is the only location where spectacular breaching activity takes place frequently enough to satisfy the tourist trade, and Great Whites can be watched without chumming. In other areas, natural predation frequency is much lower and, for reasons not fully understood, appears to occur more sub-surface. In terms of numbers, only 12 Great White Shark tourism permits have been issued; this only just manages to satisfy current tourist demand. But the clamour from tourists to see Great Whites is growing and has made the species worth more alive than dead. If chumming and the use of bait for shark viewing were abolished, this would leave just one location from which to watch Great Whites off our coasts. This would necessitate more permits being issued to cater for the demand at Seal Island, putting too much pressure on that site and interfering with Great White Shark hunting behaviour and success. In the long term, it could result in the sharks abandoning Seal Island as a feeding ground, and put an end to our viewing their spectacular breaching behaviour.

South Africa's current Great White Shark tourism model, while not ideal, is of a sound nature. Aside from observing natural predations at Seal Island in False Bay, attracting sharks with chum is the only way to carry out economically viable tourism ventures. However, the intentional feeding of Great Whites, although not proven to cause an increase in shark bites, must be curtailed and policed more effectively, as it is out of line with the ethos of responsible marine wildlife tourism in the 21st century.

APPENDIX
Avoiding Great White Shark bites

Despite the odds being extremely low that you will ever encounter a Great White Shark while surfing, diving or swimming, any marine activity undertaken along southern African coastline harbours the possibility of an unplanned encounter. Anybody who uses the same waters in which the Great White swims must understand and respect the shark's position at the top of the marine food chain, a similar position to that of lions in the terrestrial realm. While the Great White Shark can be inquisitive, it is also very cautious by nature and will often avoid confrontation by swimming away.

Below are some basic rules that will not only decrease your chances of encountering a Great White, but will also give you the know-how to ensure a safe ending for both shark and human.

General rules

- Great White Sharks, like all predators, are more likely to identify a solitary individual as potential prey, so it is wise to remain in groups in the water.
- Avoid entering the ocean when it is murky, and during darkness or twilight hours, when sharks rely on senses other than vision to locate potential prey.
- Avoid waters with known effluents or sewage, such as rivers or fishing harbours, and those used by sport or commercial fishermen, especially if signs of fish or feeding activity are observed. In fact, try to avoid any site where fish are being processed. Sighting of dolphins or porpoises does not indicate absence of sharks, as both prey on similar food resources.

- Avoid releasing any body fluids into the water (do not urinate in your wet suit). If bleeding from a wound or menstruation, avoid entering the water in the first place.
- If, while in the water, you spot a Great White Shark in the vicinity, remain calm. Alert other water-users around you, remain in or create a group, and leave the water swiftly, but in a calm and orderly manner. Then alert the local shark spotters and lifeguards.
- If you do encounter a Great White Shark close up, remain as calm as possible. Assess the situation. Do not panic. Jerky and erratic movements are likely to increase the shark's curiosity, draw it closer to you and possibly suggest injury or disease – and hence easy prey. Use any equipment (camera, surfboard, spear gun) you may be carrying to create a barrier between yourself and the shark.

Specialist tips

Scuba divers

- If you encounter a Great White Shark while scuba diving, stay on the bottom until the shark has satisfied its curiosity and moved on. It appears that the water column (the area between the sea bed and the surface) is the most dangerous place to be, and surfacing quickly in close proximity to a Great White could put the diver in an extremely dangerous situation. If in a group, stick together. On a shore dive, swim back to the land by hugging the reef and, using a compass or natural contour lines for navigation, surface as a group, back to back.

- Use the reef or wreck as a shield, especially if the Great White is displaying particularly aggressive behaviour such as swimming in tight circles, mouth gaping and making rushes towards you.
- When scuba diving with seals, be especially aware of their behaviour; when they are swimming and playing out in the open and appear relaxed it is unlikely that a Great White is around. If, however, they suddenly dart away and desert you, then be cautious, for their keen senses are likely to have picked up the presence of a Great White Shark much sooner than you.

Free divers/snorkellers

- Free divers/snorkellers are most vulnerable when on the surface or when ascending from a dive. Only dive when the water is clear enough to see the bottom, and be vigilant.
- In the Western Cape, remain within the confines of the kelp bed whenever possible. Great White Sharks are unlikely to enter dense kelp growth.

Spear fishermen

- Spear fishing off the South African coast is a high-risk activity with regard to Great White Sharks. In order to decrease the risk, don't dive and shoot fish close to Great White Shark hot spots, such as Seal island. While most of the time sharks will not bother you, the consequences of an inexperienced or foolhardy person encountering a Great White Shark while spear fishing can be fatal.
- Only shoot fish when visibility is good, so that you can see an approaching Great White from a distance and take evasive action by surrendering your fish.

- If diving from the shore, keep your fish on a long stringer or on a buoy. Ideally, one should dive from a boat to allow the removal of injured and dead fish from the water quickly.
- Use the unloaded spear gun to push away any overly curious Great White Shark; this should be enough to keep the shark at bay.
- Upon sighting a shark, release your catch immediately and slowly back away, facing the shark. No catch is worth the risk of personal injury.

Surfers/bodyboarders

- Use surfing beaches where shark spotters and trained life guards are stationed.
- Don't surf in murky water near river mouths, especially after heavy rainfall or during times of flooding.
- Don't surf in areas where bait and game fish are running, seals are feeding and seabirds are diving.
- When visiting new areas, enquire about the local conditions, and talk to local surfers, beach users and fishermen about known hot spots to avoid.

Surf skiers and kayakers

- Avoid paddling in areas known to be frequented by Great White Sharks, i.e. near seal colonies and in areas where they congregate inshore during the summer months.
- If approached by a Great White Shark, stop paddling and remain still – it is the movement of the kayak that most interests the shark. When we have encountered Great White Sharks while conducting research from kayaks, we have found that the harder and faster we paddled, the greater was the sharks' interest, and the closer they came to

the boat. Once we stopped paddling, however, most sharks circled the kayak once or twice and then lost interest.

■ Use a large kayak, for it seems that the bigger the craft, the less likely it is that a Great White Shark will risk an investigatory bite.

■ As with swimmers and divers, there seems to be safety in numbers – paddle in groups.

A Great White sneaks up from behind to investigate our research kayak, but then quickly continues on its way, disregarding our presence completely.

Great White Shark tourism in South Africa

Dyer Island

Location/how to get there
The departure point for all excursions to Dyer Island is the town of Gansbaai/Kleinbaai, which is situated about 180 km to the east of Cape Town. It can be reached in two hours by car from Cape Town on a tarred road in excellent condition. Most operators run shuttle services from Cape Town, which will pick up tourists at their hotels or hostels early in the morning, drive them to Gansbaai and then bring them back at the end of the day.

Description
During the winter months, eight operators take tourists to Dyer Island, which lies 8 km offshore; during summer, they visit a remote stretch of adjacent coast called Shark Bay. Despite the areas being relatively large, the high number of tourist boats operating here often results in their lying in close proximity to each other, competing to attract the same sharks to their boats and cages. The operation involves chumming, bait on a rope, surface viewing and cage diving.

When to go
There are two distinct seasons for watching Great Whites in this area. From February/March to August/September, all shark watching takes place in the water surrounding Dyer Island and Geyser rock (the latter is home to a large colony of Cape fur seals). The best time for shark watching at Dyer Island is from May to August, when the sharks at their most abundant (up to 25 sharks can be spotted in a single day), and the visibility is usually good and, on exceptional days, can reach 20 m. However, this period falls in the midst of the southern winter, when regular cold fronts batter the coast with monstrous waves and gale-force winds. Cage-diving days are consequently limited, and many trips are cancelled. The sharks seem to leave Dyer Island in August/September, and the boats follow them to Shark Bay, the inshore regions of the adjacent mainland coast, where they can be seen until January/February. While the summer weather tends to be much calmer, and almost every day is good for shark tourism, the water can often be extremely murky, and visibility poor. In general, shark sightings are at their yearly low between January and March, but chances of observing Great Whites remain at over 50 per cent – at least from the surface. However, none of these 'seasons' can be guaranteed, and in some years the sharks change their patterns of arrival and departure, influenced by oceanographic or ecological factors we do not yet understand.

Great White tourism operators:
Marine Dynamics:
www.marinedynamics.co.za
Shark Cage Diving:
www.sharkcagediving.net
Shark Diving Unlimited:
www.sharkdivingunlimited.co.za
Shark Lady Adventures:
www.sharklady.co.za
White Shark Adventures:
www.whitesharkdiving.com
The White Shark Diving Company:
www.sharkcagediving.co.za
White Shark Ecoventures:
www.white-shark-diving.com
White Shark Projects:
www.whitesharkprojects.co.za

Seal Island, Mossel Bay

Location/how to get there
The point of departure for all excursions to Seal Island is the town of Mossel Bay, situated some 380 km east of Cape Town – about a four-hour drive on the N2 motorway along the famous Garden Route. Alternatively, one can fly from Cape Town to George, from which it is a further 45-minute drive to Mossel Bay.

Description
The operation at Mossel Bay is run in the same manner as that at Dyer Island, involving chumming, bait on a rope, surface viewing and cage diving. Only one operator is allowed to work in the area, so that the experience feels more natural, and less like a mass tourism activity. In addition, Seal Island is located in one of the most sheltered bays along the South African coast, and the seas are almost always calm; very few trips are cancelled due to bad weather. A disadvantage, however, is that the visibility here is usually much lower than at Dyer Island.

When to go
Great White Shark tourism is available all year, apart from the peak summer holiday period, when the beaches are packed with bathers. (Sharks are present in the area whether the operator is there or not, but the temporary cessation of shark tourism is undertaken so as not to alarm holiday-makers.) The best time to embark on a trip to see Great White Sharks here is between May and September.

Great White tourism operator:
Shark Africa:
www.sharkafrica.co.za

Seal Island, False Bay

Location/how to get there:
The point of departure for all excursions to the False Bay Seal Island is Simon's Town, located near the southern tip of the Cape Peninsula, and a 45-minute drive from the centre of Cape Town.

Description
The operations at False Bay are run in a very different manner from those at Dyer Island and Seal Island in Mossel Bay. The main reason for visiting this site is not to cage dive with Great White Sharks but to observe their natural behaviour while they hunt Cape fur seals. The boats depart shortly before dawn and arrive at Seal Island, a 40-minute trip, just before daybreak, when predation of seals is most frequent. The boat drifts off the southern side of the island, and often the first thing one sees is a Great White Shark leaping clear of the water in pursuit of a seal. Sometimes, visitors are treated to dozens of predations in just a matter of hours; on such days, this parcel of ocean rates among the world's top ten wildlife-viewing spectacles.

When to go
Great White Sharks frequent Seal Island only between April and September and, outside these months, hardly any predations can be viewed. The operators then head offshore to dive with mako and blue sharks.

Great White tourism operators:
African Shark Eco-Charters:
www.ultimate-animals.com
Apex Predators:
www.apexpredators.com

FURTHER READING

Bonfil, R, Meyer, M, Scholl, MC, Johnson, R, O'Brien, S, Oosthuizen, H, Swanson, S, Kotze, D & Paterson, M. 2005. 'Transoceanic migration, spatial dynamics and population linkages of white sharks.' *Science*. 310. 5745:100-103.

Cliff, G, Dudley, SFJ & Davies, B. 1989. 'Sharks caught in the protective gill nets of Natal, South Africa. 2. The great white shark *Carcharodon carcharias* (Linnaeus).' *South African Journal of Marine Science*. 8:131-144.

Ellis, R & McCosker, JE. 1991. *Great White Shark*. Stanford University Press, Stanford. 270 pp.

Klimley, AP & Ainleu, DG. 1996. *Great White Sharks: The Biology of* Carcharodon carcharias. Academic Press, California. 517 pp.

Nel, DC & Peschak, TP (eds). 2006. *Finding a balance: White Shark conservation and recreational safety in False Bay and the Cape Peninsula, South Africa*. Proceedings of a specialist workshop. WWF South Africa Report Series – 2006/Marine/001.

Pardini, AT *et al*. 2001. 'Sex-biased dispersal of great white sharks'. *Nature*. 412:139-140.

Peschak, TP. 2005. *Currents of Contrast: life in southern Africa's two Oceans*. Struik, Cape Town. 200 pp.

Peschak, TP & Scholl, MC. 2005. 'Shark Detectives.' *Africa Geographic*. September, 36-47.

ACKNOWLEDGEMENTS

Writing and photographing *Great White Sharks* would never have been possible without the great generosity, insight and enthusiasm of many people. The following people, however, stand out and deserve a special mention: Cheryl-Samantha Owen, Ramon Bonfil, Jenna Cains, Alison Kock, Mike Meyer, Trey Snow, Geremy Cliff, Pippa Parker, Cisca Vennard, Robin Cox and Helen de Villiers. In South Africa, ORMS look after all my topside photographic needs and I wish to extend a big thank you to Mike, Andrew, Steve, Tracy, John, Vincent, Cindy and the rest of the team for often going well beyond the call of duty. In London, Steve Warren at Ocean Optics deals with all my underwater photo requirements and supplies me with great equipment and great advice. A hearfelt thank you to Deon Nel, Aaniyah Omardiem, Rob Little and Tony Frost of WWF-SA for supporting and encouraging my work to popularise and raise conservation awareness of southern Africa's oceans and coast. Most importantly, I wish to thank my parents for their love and for nurturing and encouraging my 'aquatic' lifestyle from a very early age.

Thomas P Peschak

I especially would like to thank my parents, Peter and Theres, for always supporting my endeavours to follow my dreams, and for always being there. The White Shark Trust fieldwork would not have been possible without the assistance and support of the research assistants and interns I have had over the years and, although they are too numerous to name here, I would like to thank them for all their help and assistance, and for the friendship of most of them. And, lastly, I would like to thank Sonny Gruber for being the first person to introduce me into the real world of Sharks at the Shark Lab in Bimini many years back.

Michael C Scholl

INDEX